Michel Montignac

Eat Yourself SLIM COOKBOOK

VOLUME ONE

Erica House

BALTIMORE   AMSTERDAM   SALAMANCA

ISBN: 1-893162-10-9
Library of Congress Catalog Card Number: 99-64663

PUBLISHED BY ERICA HOUSE BOOK PUBLISHERS
www.ericahouse.com
Baltimore   Amsterdam   Salamanca

Printed in the United States of America

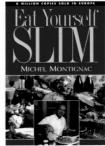

Introduction

Throughout the world, obesity is reaching epidemic proportions. Nearly two-thirds of Americans are overweight, and complications related to obesity now represent the second leading cause of death in the United States.

Founded upon a current knowledge of physiology and nutrition, with an impressive depth of scientific research at its base, the Montignac Method was a true revelation for us. We have found that a major strength of the Montignac Method is that in addition to shedding unwanted pounds, our patients develop a feeling of renewed vitality and sense of well-being not previously experienced.

With the Montignac Method, food is no longer your enemy. The _Eat Yourself Slim Cookbook_ has been created so that you can easily apply the Method in your daily cooking habits. The recipes are simple, and the choice of foods is reminiscent of the freshness of a morning at a Parisian market. Even more so, this book will introduce you to many aspects of French cuisine, not only one of the best food cultures in the world, but also one which is known to help reduce the risk of cardiovascular disease.

So keep up the good work changing your eating habits, fall in love with cooking, dare to try the different meals presented in the _Eat Yourself Slim Cookbook_, and enjoy a better quality of life!

JOHN E. KILGORE, M.D.
CHRISTINE LARAMEE, M.D.
MONTIGNAC NUTRITION AND VITALITY CENTERS

Dr. Christine Laramee, a primary care physician, has been dealing regularly with patients in whom diabetes, hyperlipidemia, cardiovascular disease, sleep apnea, and other co-morbid conditions are exacerbated by a state of obesity. Similarly, as an orthopedic surgeon, Dr. John E. Kilgore has found himself repeatedly reinforcing the importance of weight loss to overweight individuals for reducing the stress on joints, in order to improve the symptoms of arthritis.

CONTENTS

Foreword

I t took our contemporaries half a century to rediscover one of the fundamental principles of our existence: the need to have a healthy diet. Anyone who takes care of animals – breeders as well as veterinarians – knows that the survival, growth, and good health of an animal depend upon its diet and the specific nutritional quality of the diet. The epidemic known as "mad cow disease" called back to order those apprentice witch doctors who had taken dangerous liberties with their profession's code of ethics.

Since the middle of the 20th century and the advent of allopathic medicine, which is centered much more around the treatment of diseases than on their causes, humans have been forgetting that their diets have a role to play besides that of satiation or enjoyment. It is the reason for which more and more people's choices have become oriented toward standardized and prepackaged industrial foods, which are essentially practical.

In addition, the increase in the number of women in the workforce has reduced considerably the time dedicated to the preparation of family meals. More and more, culinary know-how, once passed on from mother to daughter, has fallen little by little into the forgotten remoteness of tradition. In a country like the United States, expanding mirror of our poor dietary habits, it has even become degrading for women to spend time cooking. Only those who have not been emancipated remain slaves to the stove.

This period is becoming, thank God, increasingly passé. First because for a decade, the field of neo-dietetics has done its best to show that the caloric content of food has no relative importance and that the preponderant factor, rather, is nutritional content in terms of nutriments (vitamins, mineral salts, trace elements, fiber, essential fatty acids, etc.). In effect, it is the determining factor in disease-prevention. Next because we have come to understand that food produced by agro-industrial processes risks being nutritionally stripped. And then also, it must be recognized that human mentalities have evolved toward a return to certain traditional values. This means rediscovering the pleasure of cooking, which goes along with the desire to eat more natural foods.

8

By preparing one's meals using fresh products and elementary culinary principles as often as possible, our contemporaries are going to be able to kill three birds with one stone. They will be able to eat more wholesomely to the benefit of their health (and that of their families), to indulge themselves and their immediate entourage by concocting flavorful dishes, and, finally, to contribute to the rediscovery of an art that is one of the foundations of our civilization: cuisine.

Cuisine is like love! Everything has been said about it and yet everything remains to be said, so vast and inexhaustible is the subject. Moreover, it is distinct from other artistic disciplines because cuisine is an art in and of itself. Just as in music or in painting, the culinary arts have their virtuosos to whom the stars of restaurant guides have been largely consecrated. They are there to make us dream and salivate, and they can even marvelously delight our tastebuds and fulfill our greatest gastronomic hopes if we have the financial means. We go to eat at Bernard Loiseau's for the same reasons we go to listen to Pavarotti at the Opera: we are searching for the supreme satisfaction of our senses. Great cuisine envies nothing of great music. Only the nature of the "piano" differs. Painting is created with a palette of colors, music with a range of sounds. Cuisine is created with a palette of flavors and an almost infinite range of products. Thus, it can provide a way for multiple variations to be created in function with the choices that are made.

That is why there is no one *single* kind of cuisine, but there are *several* kinds. Japanese and Chinese cuisine, as well as Italian, Spanish, Greek and Mexican, if they are well orchestrated, have never been bad compared to our noble French cuisine, even if sometimes, to us, they seem to lack depth and, often, sophistication. In reality, what makes French cuisine different from the others is its gastronomic scope.

And in the same way that one must develop a taste for opera, one must be educated in true, great gastronomy in order to appreciate it. In France, such an initiation is part of the culture. That is why in each French man and woman lies dormant a gastronome. Some remain asleep their entire lives, which is quite regrettable. Others open one eye from time to time as opportunities present themselves little by little. But everyone wakes up completely as soon as the day comes when they head for the stove. It is by "gastronomizing" that one becomes a gastronome, and by cooking that one becomes a cook! Chefs Marc Meneau and Marc Vérat even succeeded at hauling themselves up onto the Michelin Guide's three-star podium, even though they were self-taught.

But like all arts, cuisine begins with a technique; that is, with basic principles that make up its foundations. It is from that point that one constructs and can even possibly try to improvise one day. As in any discipline, success comes from one undeniable principle: rigor. Even at your level, you must do your best to be perfectionist. Perfectionist and demanding in the qualitative choice of ingredients: it is better, for example, to use frozen fish than fish that may not be fresh. Perfectionist in food preparation: nothing is more disagreeable than finding bones in a piece of fish or soil in lettuce. Perfectionist with seasoning: a dish should have neither too much nor too little seasoning, but just enough. That is why it is good, following the example of all great chefs, to constantly taste what you are cooking. Perfectionist by doing your best to serve your dishes hot. This is not only a question of organization, but also one of politeness to your guests. Perfectionist in insisting of oneself (or possibly of one's entourage) that a minimum of indispensable utensils and instruments in good condition be available. A good worker cannot work without good tools. A pianist is never made to play a piano that is out of tune. Perfectionist, finally, because it is the only way to progress and to obtain high levels of satisfaction.

Because cooking serves first and foremost to bring pleasure to yourself and, at the same time, to bring pleasure to others.

The Principles of This Book

This book was put together respecting four series of principles: dietary, health, culinary and gastronomical.

First of all, the recipes it offers conform to the Montignac Method. For those who do not yet know, this method is not a diet, but a veritable philosophy of food. It proposes a regrouping of dietary habits beginning with making choices based on nutritional criteria. In effect, it has been demonstrated that the richer foods are nutritionally, the greater their capacity to generate metabolic processes, which induce better health and prevention of weight gain. (See *Eat Yourself Slim* by the same author.)

Thus, no recipe presented here contains bad carbohydrates (sugar, white flour, potatoes, corn, non-stick white rice, etc.). In addition, we propose alternative techniques for thickening sauces. Finally, a number of possibilities are suggested for replacing the never-ending pasta, potatoes and rice which are too often present in the average diet, even though so many other foods are available to us, like excellent legumes (lentils, beans, peas, etc.) and such a varying range of vegetables that anyone's tastes could be satisfied.

The majority of the recipes in this book, furthermore, were inspired by Provençale, or more generally, Mediterranean, cooking. First because my personal tastes have always been partial to this sunshine-filled cuisine: I have always practiced it and was already recommending it in my first books in 1986. Next because living in southeastern France for several years allowed me to venture even further in my experimentation by making it a daily habit. And most importantly because it has since been officially recognized by all international health authorities that the Mediterranean dietary method is the best in the world, notably the one that is most effective in preventing cardiovascular risk and assuring optimal life expectancy.

Furthermore, several culinary options are deliberately proposed in this book. Some, if they do not surprise you, will at least cause some teeth to grind (or perhaps even incite some shoulder shrugs) among traditional chefs.

FATS AND THEIR SUBSTITUTES

The first of these options consists of forever banning butter from all cooking.

Without exception, all recipe books (those of great chefs as well as those of lesser-known cooks who also merit acknowledgement of the extent of their culinary and pedagogical talent) suggest butter as a cooking fat. Even in the great classics of Provençale cuisine, butter, paradoxically, is found in a large number of recipes.

This practice originates in the fact that butter used to be a rare, expensive product and, thus, a noble one. Cuisine made with butter, then, was a privilege shared by the rich (aristocrats, then bourgeois) and, consequently, was largely developed by the chefs who cooked for them. Thus, the French gastronomic tradition was founded essentially on cuisine made with butter.

When visiting the kitchen of great restaurants one cannot help but notice, enthroned near the stove, a large tub of oily liquid kept warm in a bain-marie: clarified butter. (Chefs "clarify" butter in order to conserve only the fat and, especially, to get rid of its "impurities", notably its yellow tint and the dark coloration it gets when heated beyond 250°F.) Clarified butter is used in all cooking and in the preparation of a large number of sauces.

Thus, you must know that while butter can be considered a beneficial food nutritionally (in the amount of 10 to 25g per day) when consumed uncooked or simply melted, this is no longer the case once it is used for cooking. Butter is formed essentially of saturated fats, composed of "short chain" fatty acids that can be broken down quickly by enzymes in the small intestine. That is why fresh butter, like that which we spread on bread, is digested without difficulty. But around 210°F, these famous short chain fatty acids are simply destroyed. Cooked butter thus becomes indigestible, because it is broken down with more difficulty by digestive enzymes, and is therefore toxic. Thus, it constitutes a supplementary potential health risk. From 250°F on, butter becomes completely altered and blackens. It forms acrolein, which has been recognized as a carcinogenic substance.

Thus, as soon as you put a pat of butter in a saucepan or pot (to make a traditional recipe), its temperature rises regularly to 320 or 350°F, which is obviously toxic for the consumer.

This is why the fat that I recommend for all cooking above 210°F is goose (or duck) fat.

Goose fat has three advantages. First, it is principally a mono-unsaturated fat. In reality, it is an oleic acid, meaning that it has the same chemical structure as olive oil, whose health benefits are well established. Next, goose fat is better than all other fats at supporting high temperatures (greater than 400°F), all in keeping intact its molecular structure. It thus remains digestible and beneficial in the cardiovascular sense, even once cooked. The last advantage of goose fat, and by no means the least of them, is that it gives an exceptional flavor to preparations, making them high-level gastronomical foods.

However, if you can't find goose fat you can use olive oil as a good substitute.

Finally, you will notice that in a large number of recipes, I often propose using **soy cream instead of regular cream.** I should note that it is a new ingredient which was not available until 1995 and which we are still discovering today with a rather favorable *a priori.* With it, one can make a creamy sauce without the disadvantages of saturated fats, which are contained in light and heavy cream. It is a product that works better with vegetables and fish. If used with meat, I suggest enhancing the flavor with a little goose fat.

The only disadvantage to soy cream (other than the fact that it is not yet easily found everywhere, except in health food stores), is that it curdles if cooked over high heat or for too long. Thus, it does not do well when simmered for a long time. Added at the end of cooking or thawing, though, it is perfect. **If soy cream is not available you can use normal dairy cream instead.**

COOKING

The other option I propose in this book is that of low-temperature cooking. Whether browning onions in a saucepan or pot, cooking vegetables, fish, seafood, or even certain meats (notably poultry), there is no need for high heat, which excessively caramelizes (and even actually burns) these foods. Because of the molecular breakdown that follows, foods cooked at high temperatures become indigestible and even toxic. This phenomenon is called the Maillard reaction. (Maillard was the first scientist to show that heat causes a chemical decomposition of the molecular structure of foods. For example, the brown pigments and the polymers that appear under the effect of a significant rise in temperature are the by-products of the breakdown of proteins and compound sugars. The new substances produced because of the cooking are considered, according to certain authors (P. Dang, 1990), toxic, peroxidic, mutagenic, even carcinogenic.)

Whenever you have difficulty digesting (notably when leaving a restaurant, even a very reputable one), you can, without much of a doubt, blame the high temperatures at which the foods you consumed were prepared. As for adverse effects on health, they will only be evident in the long term because they accumulate in infinitesimal quantities, which make an identification of the relation of the cause to the effect quite difficult.

To end the section on cooking, there is one last option that I propose for cooking with oil on the stovetop: once the food is cooked, throw away the used oil and replace it with fresh oil. It is more digestible and better for your health.

THE RECIPES

What characterizes these two hundred recipes is that they are **simple, fast, practical,** and, for 98% of them, call for **inexpensive** ingredients.

In effect, rapidity seems to have become a necessary condition in culinary elaboration today. Statistics show that we consecrate an average of about twenty minutes to the preparation of our evening meals. Many have renounced cooking themselves (buying already prepared dishes) precisely because they only have a small amount of time to devote to cooking. This book, then, should allow you to rediscover the pleasure of cooking because no proposed recipe takes longer than half an hour to prepare, the average falling around twenty minutes.

They require only that you have a minimum of culinary knowledge to carry them out, because a recipe book is not an introductory book on how to cook. Excellent examples of such books exist, and the best education one can receive in this domain is still that which one acquires "on the job" with a parent, a grandparent, or even by taking a specialized course. Such courses can be found just about everywhere.

Last but not least, an important aspect to emphasize is that this first volume of the *Eat Yourself Slim Cookbook* is inspired by the concept of **nutritional gastronomy** that I began to develop in my previous works. Until then, the dietary world was divided into two camps, in which each representative considered the frontier with an exacerbated Manicheanism. There was, on one side, the Rabelaisian world of "all you can eat", that of interminable banquets and dishes overflowing with very fatty, very tasty provisions. It was that of the jovial fellows, whose joy of living and existential well-being we measured by the puffy good-naturedness of their faces and by the fullness of their waists. It was the privileged world of gastronomy, of gourmets and gourmands who, heedlessly and philosophically, with painstakingly Epicurean and hedonistic sophistication, were digging their own tombs with their forks.

And then, on the other side there was (and still is) the puritanical and sadomasochistic world of conventional dietetics, that of interdictions, of frugal, symbolic, and above all low-calorie portions; of odorless, insipid and flavorless foods, and that of envelopes of powdered proteins and meal substitutes. It was (and still is) the world of those for whom eating is nearly a sin. It is a world of unhappy people, of killjoys and party poopers, of those who avoid eating when hungry; those who do their best to make you feel guilty, those who simply make you lose your appetite when you look at them. In other words, it is the world of those who, under the pretext of prolonging your life, quite simply keep you from living.

"Nutritional gastronomy" is an attempt at reconciling the two enemy-brothers. It is a middle ground between dietary debauchery and asceticism. It first comes from the idea that eating, besides being necessary, must be pleasurable; that it is an act that should contribute to your quality of life. It denounces all restrictive approaches leading to food privation and severely condemns all practices consisting of "fooling" hunger and yet pretending to satisfy the needs of the body by artifices such as meal substitutes, appetite cutters, and dietary supplements. Nutritional gastronomy means "eating well", "eating for pleasure", and "eating healthily". It is the return to a certain dietary good sense. It is "eating intelligently", which consists of keeping the best of gastronomical tradition while taking inspiration from current scientific knowledge on nutrition, putting into question the preconceived notions of outmoded dietetics.

Brillat-Savarin asserted that, "The destiny of the nations depends on the way in which they feed themselves." Let us bet that France will be able to keep the lead it has always had over other countries in this domain, knowing how to make its gastronomy evolve in the right direction. Moreover, an entirely new generation of great chefs has been doing so for several years.

REMINDER FOR VEGETARIANS

Many readers of Montignac books are vegetarian. In order to help them identify in one glance the recipes that are convenient to them, we put a "V" on top of the page to indicate if the recipe is a vegetarian one.

We thought it could also be helpful to mention whether the recipe is restricted to Phase II.

If nothing is mentioned regarding the phase it obviously means the recipes work for both, Phase I and Phase II.

Kitchen Ware

17

In order to cook correctly, it is obviously important to have a minimum amount of appropriate, good quality equipment at one's disposition. You should never hesitate to buy utensils that are a little bit more expensive than the others because they will last longer.

PANS

You need four: two large, one medium-sized and one small. Only choose high quality non-stick pans.

Be careful! Never use metallic utensils in such pans, but only wooden spoons or spatulas.

Same precaution for cleaning them: never use metallic sponges.

In addition, it is useful to have two or three lids of several dimensions that can also be used for the saucepans.

SAUCEPANS

A minimum of three saucepans is necessary: one large, one medium-sized and one small. Never buy aluminum saucepans (whose usage should be prohibited) because they can be toxic in the long run. Only use stainless steel saucepans with a thick base, or even true, tin-plated copper saucepans.

HIGH-SIDED FRYING PANS, STEWPOTS AND CASSEROLE DISHES

You need a large stewpot for making soups, stews, ratatouille, pasta, and large vegetables like cabbage.

You also need a high-sided frying pan with a fitted lid, which will be useful for a number of dishes.

The casserole dish, which can be made of cast iron like they used to be, allows for excellent simmering (the heat is perfectly distributed over the entire surface) and can even be used as a serving dish.

The fish kettle is also a sort of "stewpot" necessary in a number of circumstances.

BOWLS AND JATTES

These, in a way, are small, medium-sized and large "salad bowls". There can never be enough of them in a kitchen. You need at least half a dozen in all sizes. With the exception of one (large) metallic bowl to be used for double-boilers, the others can be ordinary, and thus inexpensive, made of glass or even plastic.

BAKING DISHES AND MOLDS

These are high-edged dishes that go in the oven. They can be glass or ceramic, but also stoneware, which allows them to be used as serving dishes as well. You need at least three: one very large, one medium-sized and one small.

For desserts and terrines, it will be useful to have one or two molds with an anti-stick coating.

STEAMER

I do not recommend the pressure-cooker, which is an expensive and especially dangerous utensil. First because it can hit you in the face or burn you, but especially because it cooks at a very high temperature (from 400 to 575°F). Moreover, as I already explained, the higher the cooking temperature, the more food is nutritionally stripped.

The ideal, then, is to have an ordinary two-level steamer. It is very inexpensive and will never stop surprising you. My advice is to have two: one 10-inches in diameter, and one oval for fish.

KNIVES (AND SHARPENER)

These must be of the highest quality and easy to sharpen. You need large knives, but also small and medium-sized ones. The best thing to do is to buy them all at once from a professional restaurant supplier. Such suppliers can be found in almost all cities.

BEATER-BLENDER

The ideal is to have a multi-function food processor. These are available on the market at all prices. Here again, if you can, it is always preferable to acquire high-quality equipment, close to professional material. But it is a large investment. In the meantime, you can use the everyday equipment found in all large department stores.

I advise, though, making an effort where the beater is concerned. It must be sufficiently powerful. To successfully beat egg whites until firm or make fine whipped cream, you must have a tool that spins at high speed and, if possible, is freestanding, which allows you to do other things at the same time.

THE ESSENTIALS

These are all the little instruments that are considered "accessories" but whose role is essential. They are cited in no particular order:

wooden spoons of various sizes (at least three);
a rubber spatula that will allow you to scrape the bottoms of bowls;
a brush for coating foods and for greasing cookie sheets and molds;
a skimmer;
a sieve and a strainer (one average model of each is sufficient);
two whisks (one small and one medium-sized);
two ladles (one small and one regular);
measuring cups and a scale;
several cutting boards (one small, one medium-sized and one very large);

Optional but quite useful:
"circles".
These cylinders made of metal or plastic, of various diameters
(3 ½, 4, and 5 in) and various heights (¾ to 3 ½ in),
allow you to "form" a preparation in the middle of an individual plate
for a better presentation. Generally, you allow the preparation
to set in the circles, then remove them just before serving.

Quite obviously, this list is not complete, but we will suppose that the
rest of the materials (from the grater to the mincer to the can opener) are
already part of your kitchen's inventory.

Spices and Aromatic Herbs

GOOD COMBINATIONS
OF SPICES AND AROMATIC HERBS

LAMB
Garlic, dill, curry, mint, oregano, rosemary, thyme.

BEEF
Garlic, basil, cumin, curry, ginger, bay leaves, marjoram, oregano, red pepper, Cayenne pepper, thyme.

PORK
Garlic, dill, coriander, curry, cumin, ginger, Cayenne pepper, rosemary, sage, thyme.

VEAL
Garlic, dill, coriander, bay leaves, oregano, rosemary, sage, thyme.

POULTRY
Garlic, basil, coriander, chives, curry, tarragon, ginger, bay leaves, marjoram, oregano, thyme.

EGGS
Chives, cumin, curry, tarragon, Cayenne pepper, savory.

FISH
Dill, chives, coriander, tarragon, bay leaves, nutmeg, sage, thyme.

SEAFOOD
Dill, basil, chervil, cloves, coriander, curry, tarragon, bay leaves, marjoram, oregano, red pepper, sage, thyme.

ASPARAGUS
Dill, basil, chives, tarragon, sesame seeds, nutmeg.

EGGPLANT
Garlic, basil, marjoram, oregano, red pepper, sage, thyme.

BROCCOLI, CABBAGE, CAULIFLOWER, BRUSSELS SPROUTS
Garlic, basil, cumin, curry, tarragon, ginger, marjoram, oregano, thyme.

MUSHROOMS
Garlic, dill, basil, chives, tarragon, marjoram, oregano, rosemary.

ZUCCHINI
Garlic, dill, basil, chives, tarragon, marjoram, mint, oregano.

SPINACH
Garlic, basil, tarragon, nutmeg.

BROAD BEANS
Dill, basil, chives, tarragon, marjoram, savory, sage, oregano, rosemary.

DRIED BEANS
Garlic, coriander, cumin, tarragon, marjoram, oregano, red pepper, Cayenne pepper, rosemary, savory, sage, thyme.

GREEN BEANS
Garlic, dill, basil, tarragon, bay leaves, marjoram, mint, rosemary, savory.

TURNIPS
Cinnamon, ginger, nutmeg, red pepper.

PEAS
Dill, basil, chives, tarragon, marjoram, mint, oregano, savory.

BELL PEPPERS
Garlic, chives, coriander, marjoram, oregano, thyme.

TOMATOES
Garlic, dill, chives, coriander, tarragon, marjoram, oregano, rosemary, savory, sage, thyme.

RICE
Garlic, chives, cumin, curry, tarragon, sage.

Menus for Three Months

GENERAL COMMENTS

These menus have been preferred for those who want to use the recipes in this book to lose weight and would like to know how to structure their meals over an extended period to achieve their goal.

All the dishes in the menu program conform to Phase 1 - the weight reduction phase of the Montignac Method - though the rules have been slightly relaxed for lunch on Saturdays and Sundays. Those not prepared to lose weight in a leisurely fashion should skip the desserts.

Some may be surprised to find cooked apples featuring in some of the recipes. Although they have never been excluded from Phase 1, the recommendation that raw fruit should only be eaten on an empty stomach has led some people to eliminate cooked fruit from their meals altogether.

This is to misunderstand the reason for recommending that raw fruit should be eaten on an empty stomach. The reason is quite simple: with the exception of red fruit like strawberries and raspberries, raw fruit eaten at the end of a meal or after other foods, is liable to ferment in the stomach and upset the digestive process. The advice that raw fruit should be eaten on an empty stomach and at least 20 minutes before eating other foods, has been given for reasons of personal comfort - not because eating fruit promotes weight gain.

It is important to realize that when fruit is cooked, the risk that it will ferment in the stomach is virtually non-existent. That is why certain fruits with a low glycaemic index, like apples, can be included in the program without any problems.

I would conclude by reminding everybody following the Montignac Method, that a balanced diet requires an adequate intake of good carbohydrates at breakfast time - namely, wholemeal bread (or better still, bread made with unrefined flour), sugar-free jam or cereals like muesli (without added sugar). Fresh fruit is also essential, but it must be eaten on an empty stomach and at least 20 minutes before eating anything else.

FIRST MONTH - WEEK 1

	LUNCH	DINNER

MONDAY	Lamb's lettuce salad
	Chicken breast with lemon
	    squash*
	Green beans
	Cheese
		Cream of mushroom soup
		Tomatoes stuffed with
		    integral semolina
		Yogurt

TUESDAY	Tomato salad Veal cutlet in Parma cream* Snow peas Cheese	Cheese soufflé* Green salad Yogurt
WEDNESDAY	Mushroom salad* Mackerel in white wine Endives Cheese	Cauliflower salad Over-easy eggs with country ham Plain yogurt
THURSDAY	Celery rémoulade Trout amandine Spinach purée Cheese	Cream of leek soup Integral pasta and tomato sauce Low-fat yogurt
FRIDAY	Eggplant marinade* Turkey stew* Cheese	Sorrel soup Broccoli salad amandine* Yogurt
SATURDAY	Salmon carpaccio* Curried pork roast* Brussels sprouts Cheese Boiled cinnamon apples*	Tomato consommé Integral semolina and vegetables Fat-free plain yogurt
SUNDAY	Shrimp and avocado pâté* Salmon in salt crust* Broccoli Chocolate chestnut cake*	Eggs scrambled with bell peppers* Salad Cheese

27

FIRST MONTH - WEEK 2

	LUNCH	DINNER
MONDAY	Endive salad Grilled pork Provençale* Provençale tomatoes* Cheese	Rustic quiche* Salad Whole fat yogurt
TUESDAY	Soy sprout salad Veal liver and onions* Cheese	Cucumbers in low-fat yogurt Integral rice in tomato sauce Applesauce
WEDNESDAY	Chilled cucumber soup Filet of salmon grilled in tamari sauce* Broccoli Cheese	Mussels in soy cream* Green salad Whole fat yogurt
THURSDAY	Farandole of bell peppers and Canadian bacon* Bourguignon* Celery root purée Yogurt	Tagliatelli in a mushroom purée Low-fat plain yogurt
FRIDAY	Avocado Chicken breast à la Provençale* Green salad Cheese	Tortilla à la Montignac* Green salad Whole fat yogurt
SATURDAY	Au gratin onions* Cod Provençale* Steamed leeks* Cheese	Cream of leek soup* Provençale calamari* Crème caramel made with fructose*
SUNDAY	Lump fish terrine Scallops with shallots and soy* Lettuce farandole* Bavarian apricots with their sauce*	Sorrel brouillade* Green salad Cheese

28

FIRST MONTH - WEEK 3

	LUNCH	DINNER
MONDAY	Mussel salad Parcel of tarragon chicken breast* Endives Cheese	Leek clafoutis* Green salad Baked apples
TUESDAY	Endive salad Paprika veal* Cheese	Integral spaghetti in tomato sauce Low-fat yogurt
WEDNESDAY	Leeks in vinaigrette Grilled tuna Ratatouille* Cheese	Fish soup Tarragon soft-boiled eggs* Warm goat cheese salad
THURSDAY	Cream of mushroom soup Bordelaise rib steak* Green beans Cheese	Grated carrots in lemon juice Lentils in tomato sauce Fat-free plain yogurt
FRIDAY	Chicken salad* Eggs scrambled with bell peppers* Cheese	Ham with zucchini and parmesan* Green salad Soy "yogurt"
SATURDAY	Rémoulade of celery root and avocado* Escalope rolled in Provençale ham* Salad Mixed berry mousse*	Provençale chicken Green salad Yogurt
SUNDAY	Oysters Cornish hen in a bag Celery root purée Bitter chocolate cake*	Cream of garlic soup* Provençale poached eggs* Salad Cheese

29

FIRST MONTH - WEEK 4

	LUNCH	DINNER
MONDAY	Radishes Tuna in tomato brandade* Endive salad Cheese	Vegetable soup Chicken liver terrine* Salad Plain yogurt
TUESDAY	Heart of palm Veal cutlet in Parma cream* Cauliflower purée Cheese	Cream of broccoli soup Brown rice with tomato sauce Low-fat yogurt
WEDNESDAY	Mushroom salad* Octopus with onions* Yogurt	Cauliflower soup Zucchini and leek flan* Cheese

THURSDAY	Red cabbage salad with
	    walnuts*
	Thinly sliced veal*
	Braised endives*
	Cheese
		Grated carrots in lemon
		    juice
		Integral pasta with tomato
		    and basil sauce
		Low-fat yogurt

FRIDAY	Avocado in vinaigrette Mustard pork chops* Braised endives* Cheese	Mushroom omelet Salad Yogurt

SATURDAY	Marinated salmon
	Montignac blanquette of
	    veal*
	Peaches with cheese and
	    raspberries*
		Creamy mussel soup*
		Basquaise sea bream*
		Steamed leeks*
		Cheese

SUNDAY	Salad of jellied gizzards Roast cutlet* Mushrooms with parsley Fresh almond mousse*	Tomato flan* Salad Applesauce

SECOND MONTH - WEEK 1

	LUNCH	DINNER
MONDAY	Cauliflower in vinaigrette Garlic chicken* Grated celery root* Cheese	Tomato consommé* Vegetable couscous Low-fat yogurt
TUESDAY	Marinated mushrooms Curried pork roast* Brussels sprouts Cheese	Cretan feta terrine* Cheese omelet* Green salad Yogurt
WEDNESDAY	Greek salad (tomato + feta) Cretan lemon sole* Spinach Cheese	Fresh mint tabouleh Salad Applesauce
THURSDAY	Green bean and baby onion salad Steak tartare Cheese	Cabbage soup Integral spaghetti with zucchini Low-fat yogurt
FRIDAY	Walnut endive salad Provençale lamb medallions* Parsleyed mushrooms* Yogurt	Tuna in garlic vinegar* Eggplant au gratin* Cheese
SATURDAY	Bacon watercress salad* Bass grilled with fennel* Braised leeks* Citronnier*	Green salad with pine nuts Provençale poached eggs* Yogurt
SUNDAY	Dublin bay prawns with mayonnaise Orange duck cutlet* Framboisier*	Cream of watercress soup Artichokes in vinaigrette Cheese

31

SECOND MONTH - WEEK 2

	LUNCH	DINNER
MONDAY	Bacon frisée salad Provençale stew* Celery root purée* Cheese	Cream of tomato soup* Integral pasta with mushrooms Salad Low-fat yogurt
TUESDAY	Heart of palm Pork roast Eggplant Cheese	Cheese soufflé* Green salad Applesauce
WEDNESDAY	Warm goat cheese salad* Grilled Mediterranean prawns Creamed spinach Feta	Shallot soy cream* Provençale chicken breast* Salad Yogurt
THURSDAY	Tuna tartare* Olive cutlet* Salad Cheese	Grated carrots Curried brown rice Low-fat yogurt
FRIDAY	Radishes Turkey cutlet in cream sauce* Braised zucchini Cheese	Mimosa eggs with tuna* Warm goat cheese salad
SATURDAY	Provençale cheese mousse* Salmon sole filets* Broccoli Coffee mousse*	Cream of shrimp soup* Filet of bass in shallot sauce* Spinach Yogurt
SUNDAY	Scallops au gratin in their shells* Chicken with peas Raspberry Catalina cream*	Onion soup Mushroom-stuffed tomatoes Cheese

32

SECOND MONTH · WEEK 3

	LUNCH	DINNER
MONDAY	Almond broccoli salad* Pork loin with turnips* Cheese	Fat-free vegetable bouillon Tagliatelli with mushroom purée Low-fat yogurt
TUESDAY	Tomato and cucumber salad Beef carpaccio* Green salad Cheese	Provençale cheese mousse* Chicken breast brochette Salad Yogurt

WEDNESDAY	Green bean salad
	 Filet of sole in soy cream*
	 Cheese
		Fat-free leek soup
		 White beans with tomato
		 Low-fat yogurt mixed with
		   sugar-free fruit
		   marmalade

THURSDAY	Bacon frisée salad Grilled cutlet Salsify Cheese	Cream of watercress soup Chicken liver terrine with leeks* Plain yogurt
FRIDAY	Avocado with baby shrimp Provençale cod* Steamed leeks Cheese	Tomato consommé* Integral spaghetti with basil Low-fat yogurt
SATURDAY	Bacon broad bean salad* Fish and seafood cooked in a court-bouillon* Raspberry Catalina cream	Octopus with onions* Country apple cake

SUNDAY	Parcels of smoked salmon
	   mousse*
	 Filet of red mullet in cream
	   sauce*
	 Green bean purée
	 Flambéed Calvados apple
	   soufflé*
		Cream of mushroom soup
		 Sorrel brouillade*
		 Green salad
		 Plain yogurt with herbs

33

SECOND MONTH - WEEK 4

	LUNCH	DINNER
MONDAY	Cucumber salad Turkey with apple* Plain yogurt	Low-fat cream of asparagus soup White beans with tomato Low-fat yogurt mixed with fruit marmalade
TUESDAY	Walnut endive salad Grilled salmon steak Green beans Cheese	Sorrel soup* Chicken liver terrine* Green salad Yogurt
WEDNESDAY	Onions au gratin* Tomato brandade tuna* Cheese	Chilled cream of cucumber soup* Rustic quiche* Green salad
THURSDAY	Celery root rémoulade* Provençale filet of mutton* Ratatouille* Cheese	Fish soup Trout amandine* Salad Plain yogurt
FRIDAY	Salade niçoise Olive cutlet* Provençale tomatoes* Cheese	Tomato consommé* Integral pasta with bell pepper purée Plain yogurt with herbs
SATURDAY	Smoked salmon Roast beef Green beans Pears Belle-Hélène (Pears drizzled with chocolate)	Cream of soy with shallots* Artichokes Yogurt
SUNDAY	Scallops with dill marinade* Fillet of red mullet in cream sauce* Steamed broccoli Fresh almond mousse*	Over-easy eggs with country ham* Salad Yogurt

THIRD MONTH - WEEK °1

	LUNCH	DINNER
MONDAY	Cauliflower salad Garlic chicken* Braised fennel* Cheese	Cream of asparagus soup Vegetable couscous Low-fat yogurt
TUESDAY	Frisée with bacon Grilled black pudding Apples and cinnamon Cheese	Cream of garlic soup* Tarragon chicken breast Green salad Plain yogurt
WEDNESDAY	Tomato and feta salad Filet of sole Eggplant purée Plain yogurt	Tortilla à la Montignac Green salad Yogurt
THURSDAY	Red cabbage salad Paprika veal* Braised turnips Cheese	Tomato consommé* Tagliatelli with mushroom purée Low-fat yogurt
FRIDAY	Bavarian avocados* Swordfish brochettes Ratatouille* Cheese	Sauerkraut soup* Thinly sliced veal* Braised endives Baked apples
SATURDAY	Parcels of smoked salmon mousse* Rosemary leg of lamb Green beans Nectarines au gratin*	Fish soup Provençale calamari Salad Cheese

SUNDAY	Zucchini and bell pepper
	   flan*
	Provençale tournedos*
	Parsleyed mushrooms*
	Crème caramel made with
	   fructose
		Eggs scrambled with
		   shrimp*
		Salad
		Cheese

35

THIRD MONTH - WEEK 2

	LUNCH	DINNER
MONDAY	Bacon frisée salad Partridge with cabbage* Cheese	Grated carrots with lemon juice Lentils with tomato Low-fat yogurt
TUESDAY	Soy germ salad Basil veal liver* Braised endives* Cheese	Cheese omelet Salad Yogurt
WEDNESDAY	Tomatoes and mozzarella Fresh sardines in Xérès vinegar* Steamed broccoli Cheese	Pistou soup* Plain yogurt
THURSDAY	Green bean salad* Bordelaise rib steak* Bell pepper purée* Cheese	Tomatoes stuffed with integral semolina Low-fat yogurt
FRIDAY	Cucumber salad Duck with olives Tomato flan* Cheese	Marinated eggplant* Over-easy eggs and country ham* Cheese
SATURDAY	Scallop timbale* English leg of lamb* Broccoli Coffee mousse*	Andalou gaspacho Sorrel turbot* Salade Apricot soup*
SUNDAY	Provençale cheese mousse* Fennel turbot* Green salad* Cherry clafoutis*	Sorrel brouillade* Salad Yogurt

THIRD MONTH - WEEK 3

	LUNCH	DINNER

MONDAY	Heart of palm
	Turkey cutlet in cream
	  sauce*
	Cheese
		Cream of leek soup
		Stuffed zucchini with sour
		  cream
		Yogurt

TUESDAY	Endive salad Peppered steak Green bean purée Cheese	Avocado Chicken à la Provençale* Salad Yogurt
WEDNESDAY	Leeks in vinaigrette Filet of hake Spinach purée* Cheese	Low-fat cream of mushroom soup Curried brown rice* Salad with lemon juice Herbed fat-free plain yogurt
THURSDAY	Red cabbage in vinaigrette Provençale brochettes Cheese	Watercress soup Cretan lemon sole* Brussels sprouts Yogurt

FRIDAY	Parsleyed mushrooms*
	Chicken liver
	Green beans
	Cheese
		Tomato consommé*
		Kidney beans and artichoke
		  hearts in fat-free sour
		  cream
		Low-fat yogurt

SATURDAY	Asparagus Coq au vin* Sauerkraut Pears au vin*	Onions au gratin* Tarragon jellied eggs* Salad Cheese

SUNDAY	Scallops in dill marinade*
	Flambéed guinea fowl with
	  endives*
	Blanc-manger in rasberry
	  sauce*
		Fresh integral pasta with
		  basil tomato sauce
		Low-fat yogurt

37

THIRD MONTH - WEEK 4

	LUNCH	DINNER
MONDAY	Warm goat cheese green salad* Mustard pork chops* Braised fennel* Cheese	Chilled cream of cucumber soup* Artichokes in vinaigrette Yogurt
TUESDAY	Heart of palm Salt pork Old-fashioned cabbage* Cheese	Leek clafoutis* Green salad Plain yogurt
WEDNESDAY	Radishes Filet of whiting Green beans Cheese	Low-fat lentil soup Tomatoes stuffed with integral semolina* Herbed fat-free plain yogurt
THURSDAY	Greek marinated mushrooms Montignac veal blanquette* Cheese	Shrimp cocktail Tuna in garlic vinegar* Salad Yogurt
FRIDAY	Cauliflower salad Basil veal liver* Provençale tomatoes Cheese	Soy cream with shallots* Tomato flan* Green salad Yogurt
SATURDAY	Onions au gratin* Cockerel with sauerkraut* Bavarian raspberries with their sauce*	Sorrel soup* Trout amandine* Broccoli salad Cheese
SUNDAY	Gourmand salad* Salmon in salt crust* Endives in cream sauce* Pears au gratin*	Integral spaghetti with tomato sauce Low-fat yogurt

38

Cocktail Snacks and Dips

One of the fundamental recommendations of the Montignac Method is that alcohol should never be consumed on an empty stomach.

The Golden Rule is that first you should eat and then drink.

Here then a few suggestions how to satisfy what should be a responsibility, even for those who have no weight problem.

Snacks for those on Phase 1

- slices of smoked sausage
- salami
- chorizos
- rolled cooked ham
- rolled cured ham
- rolled smoked salmon
- green olives
- black olives
- cheese cubes
- raw vegetables (carrots, cauliflower sprigs, celery stalks,chicory leaves)
- radishes, tomatoes, cherries

Snacks for those on Phase 2

- canapé from pain intégrale (bread made from unrefined flour), with foie gras, smoked salmon, caviar or potted goose
- crab sticks
- bacon rolled on asparagus sticks

Celery and Roquefort Butter

PREPARATION: 5 MINUTES
NO COOKING

INGREDIENTS:
5 oz. Roquefort cheese
2 oz. soft butter
1 large celery stalk
4 tablespoons reduced fat (15%) sour cream
3 teaspoons Armagnac
salt, freshly ground pepper

Wash the stalk of celery. Remove the leaves and threads. Cut into lengths.

Purée the celery, butter, Roquefort, sour cream and Armagnac in a blender. Season to taste.

Spread the mixture on chicory leaves or prepared raw vegetables.

Arrange on a serving dish.

Cocktail Sauce with Roquefort

PREPARATION: 5 MINUTES
NO COOKING

INGREDIENTS:
4 oz. Roquefort cheese
4 oz. plain yogurt
2 tablespoons chopped
    parsley
freshly ground pepper

42

Crumble the Roquefort with a fork.

In a bowl, mix the cheese with the yogurt to obtain a rich cream.

Add the chopped parsley and pepper.

Serve in a bowl.

Cucumber Mousse with Fresh Goat's Cheese

PREPARATION: 10 MINUTES
NO COOKING

INGREDIENTS:

9 oz. goat's cheese - well drained

1 cucumber

2 tablespoons olive oil

1 tablespoon brown mustard

3 tablespoons chopped chives

salt, freshly ground pepper

Peel the cucumber. Slice in half, lengthwise. Remove the seeds and dice the flesh. Leave to drain for 30 minutes.

Purée the goat's cheese, cucumber, olive oil and mustard in a blender. Fold in the chopped chives and season to taste.

Chill and keep in the refrigerator until required.

NOTE:

If following Phase 1, exclude mustard from the recipe.

Ham Mousse with Avocado

PREPARATION: 5 MINUTES
NO COOKING

INGREDIENTS:
5 oz. cooked ham with
    fat removed

2 oz. cured ham with fat
    removed

2 ripe avocados

1 tablespoon olive oil

3 tablespoons sour cream

1 tablespoon cognac

juice of ½ lemon

salt, freshly ground
    pepper and tabasco

Cut the avocados into halves and remove the flesh.

Put the avocado, chopped ham, olive oil, lemon juice, cognac, sour cream, dash of tabasco, salt and pepper in the mixer and beat until creamy.

Serve chilled.

Pepper and Cheese Cocktail Sauce

PREPARATION: 5 MINUTES
NO COOKING

INGREDIENTS:

14 oz. cottage cheese
2 cloves garlic - puréed
1 bunch parsley
1 bunch chervil
1 bunch dill
20 black olives - stones removed
½ teaspoon paprika
1 tablespoon olive oil
salt, freshly ground pepper

Drain the cottage cheese through a cheesecloth. Purée in a blender with the crushed garlic, chopped parsley, chives, dill, chopped black olives, pepper and olive oil.

Season to taste.

Place in the refrigerator for at least 2 hours.

Serve as a sauce to be eaten with raw vegetables.

Tomato Cocktail Sauce

PREPARATION: 5 MINUTES
NO COOKING

INGREDIENTS:
6 oz. full milk yogurt
3 tablespoons tomato
  sauce
1 clove garlic - crushed
1 tablespoon olive oil
2 teaspoons thyme
salt, freshly ground
  pepper, cayenne

In a bowl combine the yogurt, tomato sauce and olive oil to make a uniform, creamy mixture.

Add the garlic and thyme. Stir well.

Season with salt, pepper and cayenne. Store in the refrigerator for 2 or 3 hours before serving.

46

Tuna Mousse

PREPARATION: 10 MINUTES
NO COOKING

INGREDIENTS:
9 oz. tuna in brine
1 small tin of anchovies in olive oil
5 oz. green olives - stones removed
4 tablespoons olive oil
3 cloves garlic - crushed
3 teaspoons balsamic vinegar
3 teaspoons brown mustard
1 tablespoon sour cream
freshly ground pepper

Drain the tuna and break down with a fork.

Put the tuna, anchovies and their oil, green olives, garlic, vinegar, mustard and sour cream in the blender.

Add pepper and blend until the mixture is smooth. Adjust the seasoning to taste.

Serve chilled.

47

Starters

49

Eggplant Marinade

PREPARATION: 5 MINUTES
COOKING TIME: 20 MINUTES

INGREDIENTS:
4 eggplants
2 cloves garlic
5 fl.oz. olive oil
Herbs de Provence
salt, freshly ground
    pepper, cayenne
    pepper

This dish may be eaten on its own or with other hors-d'oeuvre.

Cut the eggplants into round slices at least ½ in. thick.

Cook in a steamer for 20 minutes and allow to drain.

Make a marinade in a bowl by combining the olive oil, crushed garlic, salt, freshly ground pepper and cayenne pepper.

In a stoneware dish, layer the slices of eggplants, brushing each layer with the marinade and dusting liberally with Herb de Provence.

Make certain the layers of eggplants are pressed down well before covering the dish with plastic film and placing it in the refrigerator, where it can be kept for several days.

Aumônière with Smoked Salmon Mousse

PREPARATION: 20 MINUTES
NO COOKING

SERVES: 4

INGREDIENTS:
16 slices of smoked salmon
7 oz. sour cream
7 fl.oz. whipping cream
1 tablespoon chopped dill
1 tablespoon chopped chives
chive stalks
parsley sprigs
pepper

Line a teacup or ramekin with a generous slice of salmon and fill with the mousse.

The edges of the salmon are then tied together with a strand of chive to make an Aumônière, or pouch.

Reserve the 8 most attractive slices of smoked salmon to make the pouches.

Place the rest of the smoked salmon in a blender to make the purée.

Whip the cream in a large bowl after adding a pinch of salt.

Fold the whipped cream into the salmon purée, adding at the same time, half the dill and half the chopped chives.

Add pepper to taste.

Make the pouches using a teacup or ramekin, fill with the mousse and secure with two or three whole chive stalks.

Serve on a plate, decorate with the remaining herbs, parsley sprigs an salmon mousse.

51

Avocado Bavarois

PREPARATION: 15 MINUTES
NO COOKING

SERVES: 5

INGREDIENTS:
4 ripe avocados
   the juice of 1½ lemons
10 oz. cottage cheese - strained
2 oz. black olives, stones removed
1½ tablespoon chopped fresh parsley
1 tablespoon chopped dill
1 tablespoon olive oil
salt, freshly ground pepper, ground coriander
cayenne pepper - 1 or 2 pinches

Mix the flesh of the avocados in a blender with the lemon juice, parsley, dill, black olives, salt, pepper, coriander and cayenne pepper.

Transfer to a bowl and mix together with the cottage cheese that has been well strained.

Adjust the seasoning to taste.

Pour the mixture into a mold or individual pastry rings and leave to set in the refrigerator for 4 to 5 hours.

Unmold and serve on a bed of lettuce. Decorate with parsley and some olives.

52

Avocado Pâté with Prawns

PREPARATION: 15 MINUTES
COOKING TIME: 2 MINUTES

SERVES: 4

INGREDIENTS:
5 ripe avocados
9 oz. prawns - peeled
the juice of 2 lemons
½ oz. agar-agar
3 tablespoons
  Montbazillac (white
  semi-sweet wine from
  the Bergerac)
1 teaspoon ground green
  peppercorns
salt, cayenne pepper

Pat the prawns dry.

Mix the avocado flesh with the lemon juice and the ground green peppercorns.

Dissolve the agar-agar in the wine by warming gently.

Season with salt and cayenne pepper and mix well.

Pour into a mold and pat down well.

Place in the refrigerator for at least 6 hours.

Serve on a bed of lettuce with a light mayonnaise.

53

Beef Carpaccio

PREPARATION: 10 MINUTES
NO COOKING

Serves: 4

Ingredients:
10 oz. Carpaccio
  olive oil
granular sea salt
freshly ground pepper
Herbs de Provence

54

Carpaccio is prepared from raw beef, either top-rump or fillet, which has been finely sliced on a butcher's slicing machine. Ask your butcher to interleave the slices with greaseproof paper to prevent the slices from sticking together.

If preparing the meat at home, freeze briefly before slicing, to make it firm and easier to handle.

Arrange the Carpaccio on large plates.

Brush with olive oil.

Sprinkle lightly with the Herbs de Provence, coarse sea salt and pepper from the pepper mill.

Allow to stand and marinate for 10 to 15 minutes before serving.

Variation:

Replace Herbs de Provence with flakes of Parmesan cheese thinly pared with a potato peeler.

Cheese and Onion Rösti with Bacon

PREPARATION: 15 MINUTES
COOKING TIME: 20 MINUTES

SERVES: 4

INGREDIENTS:
8 onions
14 oz. grated Gruyère
  cheese
8 slices bacon
olive oil
freshly ground pepper

Peel and chop the onions.

In a large pan, combine olive oil and the chopped onions and heat gently to a golden brown. Season with freshly ground pepper.

Degrease the onions by turning the onions onto absorbent kitchen paper.

In individual oven-proof dishes make beds of onion and cover each portion with 3½ oz. of Gruyère cheese.

Cover each with 2 slices of bacon and place 4 in. below the grill in a very hot oven, preheated to 500°F.

Take out and serve when the cheese is lightly browned.

55

Cheese Soufflé

PREPARATION: 25 MINUTES
COOKING TIME:20 MINUTES

SERVES: 4

INGREDIENTS:
6 eggs
7 oz. grated cheese
4 tablespoons sour cream

56

Separate the yolks from the whites into two large bowls.

Mix the yolks and the grated cheese into a smooth cream. Season with salt and pepper to taste.

Lightly beat the sour cream and stir into the egg and cheese mixture.

Add a pinch of salt to the egg whites and beat until stiff. Fold delicately into the egg and cream mixture using a spatula.

Pour into an oiled soufflé dish.

Place into a preheated oven (375°F).

Raise the temperature of the oven (500°F) to ensure the soufflé rises and turns golden brown.

If you have a window in your oven, monitor the progress of the soufflé. Do not open the oven door until the soufflé reaches its optimum consistency and color after about 20 minutes.

Serve immediately. A hot soufflé should never be kept waiting!

Chicken Liver Terrine

PREPARATION: 30 MINUTES
COOKING TIME: 1 HOUR 5 MINUTES

SERVES: 5/6

INGREDIENTS:
1½ lb. chicken livers
3 chopped onions
4 cloves crushed garlic
18 oz. button
   mushrooms
7 fl.oz. whipping cream
5 egg yolks
olive oil
goose fat
Herbs de Provence
Salt, freshly ground
   pepper, cayenne
   pepper

Trim the livers and brown in a non-stick pan cooking gently for a few minutes in goose fat. Season with salt, pepper, cayenne and Herbs de Provence. Reserve.

Clean and chop the mushrooms. Heat olive oil in the pan, brown and sweat the mushrooms over a gentle heat. Pour off the water that is released during cooking.

At the same time, in another pan heat olive oil and brown the chopped onions over a gentle heat.

Place the livers, mushrooms and onions (without their cooking juices) in a large bowl. Add the garlic, whipping cream and egg yolks. Season with salt, freshly ground pepper and cayenne. Put into a blender and reduce to a fine pulp.

Pour into an ovenware dish and dust with Herbs de Provence.

Put into a warm oven (320°F) for 45 minutes.

Serve in slices on a bed of lettuce, adding some gherkins.

57

Chicken Liver and Leek Terrine

PREPARATION: 30 MINUTES
COOKING TIME: 50 MINUTES

SERVES: 4/5

INGREDIENTS:
10 leek whites
1½ lb. chicken livers
4 chopped shallots
1 envelope of gelatin
    powder
½ glass of sherry
goose fat
3 fl.oz. chicken stock
olive oil
salt, freshly ground
    pepper, cayenne
    pepper

58

Cook the leek whites in the chicken stock for 30 minutes. Strain and reserve the leeks.

Reserve the stock.

In a pan containing 1 tablespoon of goose fat, sauté the chicken livers and chopped shallots over a gentle heat. Season with salt, ground pepper and cayenne. Deglaze gently using the sherry vinegar.

Line the bottom of the earthenware terrine with leek whites.

Fill the terrine with alternate layers of chicken livers and the remaining leeks.

Dissolve the gelatin in 7 fl.oz. of the remaining stock.

Cover the terrine with the lukewarm jelly before it begins to set. Press down well and place in the fridge for 5 or 6 hours.

Turn out of the terrine and cut into slices ½ in. thick.

Serve on a bed of lettuce.

Zucchini and Sweet Pepper Flan

PREPARATION: 25 MINUTES
COOKING TIME: 1 HOUR 5 MINUTES

SERVES: 6

INGREDIENTS:
2¼ lb. zucchinis

4 red peppers

14 oz. cottage cheese - strained

5 eggs

2 oz. grated Gruyère cheese

3½ oz. double cream

nutmeg

Herbs de Provence

salt, freshly ground pepper, olive oil

Cut each zucchini into three parts, lengthwise. Cook in a steamer for 20 minutes. Reserve and drain, pressing gently to extract as much liquid as possible.

Cut the sweet peppers into halves. Remove the pith and the seeds. Place the peppers skin side up, under the grill in the oven until the skin bubbles and is slightly charred. This will make removal of the skin much easier and improve the flavor of the peppers. Peel and cut into large strips.

In a bowl, beat the eggs and then blend with the strained cottage cheese, nutmeg, Herbs de Provence and whipping cream. Salt and pepper to taste.

On the bottom of a cake tin coated with olive oil, spread out the vegetables, cover with the mixture and sprinkle with the grated Gruyère cheese.

Cook for 45 minutes in a very cool oven (260°F).

Allow to cool completely and then place in the refrigerator for 6 hours.

Remove from the tin, cut into slices and drizzle fresh olive oil over the top. Serve on a bed of lettuce.

Cretan Style Feta Terrine

PREPARATION: 30 MINUTES
COOKING TIME: 15 MINUTES

SERVES: 6

INGREDIENTS:

1 lb. genuine Greek Feta cheese

3 red peppers

3 cloves crushed garlic

3 tablespoons freshly chopped basil, together with 20 or so whole basil leaves

2 leaves gelatin (or some agar-agar)

7 fl.oz. olive oil

3½ fl.oz. full-fat sour cream

10 pitted, finely sliced black olives

1 tablespoon balsamic vinegar

salt, freshly ground pepper

fresh thyme

bunch of parsley

Slice the peppers in half. Remove the pith and the seeds. Place under the grill skin side up until the skin bubbles and chars. Remove the skin and cut the pepper into strips ½ in. wide.

Put the Feta cheese into a bowl and crush with the back of a spoon, mixing thoroughly with the olive oil at the same time. Add salt to taste. Add freshly ground pepper liberally.

Soften the gelatin leaves in cold water. Gently heat the sour cream (without bringing to the boil). Squeeze the gelatin to remove excess water, add to the warm pan and dissolve, stirring gently. Incorporate the Feta cheese.

Put the crushed garlic cloves, balsamic vinegar, freshly chopped basil, fresh thyme, sliced olives into a bowl and mix into a smooth paste.

Line a suitable cake pan with plastic film, adding alternate layers of cheese and peppers. Include two layers of basil leaves as the layers are built up to fill the tin.

Place in a refrigerator for at least 6 hours.

Cut into slices and serve on individual plates decorated with basil and parsley leaves.

Fresh Sardines with Sherry Vinegar

PREPARATION: 30 MINUTES
NO COOKING

SERVES: 4

INGREDIENTS:
2¼ lb. fresh sardines
4 crushed shallots
4 or 5 bay leaves
1 glass sherry vinegar
olive oil
coarse sea salt, freshly
ground pepper

Prepare the sardines: scale and gut under running water and remove the heads.

Remove the fillets by pulling along the backbone. Rinse and place in a shallow dish.

Mix the vinegar with the crushed shallots and cover the sardines. Lay the bay leaves flat on the sardines. Sprinkle 1 heaped tablespoon of coarse sea salt over the top.

Allow to marinade for 4 hours.

Once marinated, rinse the sardine fillets under the faucet and lay them out to dry on absorbent kitchen paper.

Arrange the fillets in a shallow dish, sprinkle with olive oil and season liberally with freshly ground pepper. Decorate with lemon slices and serve.

61

Marinated Goat's Cheese with Fresh Broad Beans

PREPARATION: 20 MINUTES
COOKING TIME: 2 MINUTES

SERVES: 4

INGREDIENTS:
4 small goat's cheeses or 4 slices, weighing about 10 oz. in all
4 fl.oz. olive oil
1 lb. fresh broad beans
4 teaspoons balsamic vinegar
1 teaspoon Herbs de Provence
1 clove garlic - crushed
salt, pepper freshly ground, cayenne pepper

Halve or quarter the four portions of cheese. Place them in a deep dish and sprinkle with the Herbs de Provence.

Mix the olive oil and crushed garlic in a bowl, lightly dusting with cayenne pepper and freshly ground pepper.

Pour the marinade over the cheese, cover with plastic film and allow to marinate for a few hours.

Shell the beans. Plunge them into boiling salted water for 2 minutes and then remove the fine skin covering them.

Place the pieces of cheese on the plates, together with the beans.

Coat with a vinaigrette made from 4 tablespoons of the marinade mixed with the balsamic vinegar. Then serve.

Monkfish Terrine

PREPARATION: 25 MINUTES
COOKING TIME: 60 MINUTES

SERVES: 6

INGREDIENTS:
3¼ lb skinned and
    filtered monkfish

8 eggs

3½ fl.oz. light cream

2 tablespoons tomato
    sauce

1 tablespoon finely
    chopped tarragon

2 fl.oz. brandy

Bouillon stock

1 lemon

salt, freshly ground
    pepper, cayenne

homemade mayonnaise

1 teaspoon tomato sauce

63

Poach the monkfish for 12 minutes in the bouillon stock with the lemon juice.

Lift out the pan and dry well on a tea towel. Cut the fillets into rectangular pieces.

Beat the eggs with the tomato concentrate and the light cream. Add salt, freshly ground pepper, cayenne pepper, tarragon and the brandy.

Place the monkfish in a lightly buttered tin and cover with the egg mixture.

Place the tin into a double-boiler before putting into a preheated oven (320°F) for 45 minutes. To make certain that the fish is cooked, pierce with the point of a knife.

Allow to cool before placing in the refrigerator for at least 5 or 6 hours.

When required, turn out of mold and cut into slices. Serve on individual plates on a bed of lettuce and decorate with a blend of homemade mayonnaise and 1 teaspoon tomato sauce.

Provençale Cheese Mousse

PREPARATION: 25 MINUTES
NO COOKING

SERVES: 4

INGREDIENTS:
14 oz. cottage cheese - strained
1 large cucumber
2 egg whites
2 tablespoons chopped chives
2 tablespoons chopped parsley
2 tablespoons olive oil
2 cloves garlic - crushed
2 teaspoons brown mustard

64

Prepare 4 flan rings about 3 in. in diameter.

Cut the cucumber into thin slices. Salt and drain.

Whisk the egg whites until stiff.

In a bowl, mix the strained cottage cheese with the whisked egg whites, chopped parsley and chives, the olive oil, mustard and crushed garlic cloves. Salt and pepper to taste.

Place the rings on individual plates. Line the bottom and sides of the rings with the cucumber slices. Fill with the mixture. Cover with the remaining slices and place in the fridge for 3 hours.

Remove the rings and decorate with parsley or lettuce and drizzle with olive oil before serving.

Scallops Marinated with Dill

PREPARATION: 15 MINUTES
NO COOKING

SERVES: 4

INGREDIENTS:
4 to 6 scallops per
 person
fine sea salt
1 bunch dill
freshly ground pepper
olive oil

Put the scallops on a plate so that they do not touch each other and place in the freezer for 15 to 20 minutes so that they become firm without freezing solid.

Take a very sharp knife and finely slice the scallops.

Cover each plate with the scallop slices so they partially overlap each other like the scales of a fish.

Sprinkle with sea salt and pepper. Drizzle with olive oil, spreading lightly all over the sliced scallops with a brush.

Sprinkle with finely chopped dill.

Cover with plastic film and allow to marinate at least 30 minutes before serving.

65

Scallop Timbales

PREPARATION: 25 MINUTES
COOKING TIME: 60 MINUTES

SERVES: 4

INGREDIENTS:
4 large scallops with
coral (or 8 small ones)
1½ pints lobster bisque
3 egg yolks + 2 whole
eggs
7 fl.oz. double cream
salt, freshly ground
pepper

66

The timbales may be kept in the refrigerator and reheated at the last moment in a microwave or in a very cool oven set at 210°F.

Separate the scallops from their corals.

Blend the coral with the double cream.

Heat the lobster bisque without causing it to boil.

Add the coral cream and continue cooking for 2 minutes. Remove from heat and allow to stand for 10 minutes. Reserve a third mixture, which will be used later for the sauce.

In a big bowl, beat 2 eggs together with 2 yolks. Add the two-thirds of the prepared mixture to the beaten eggs, whipping continuously.

Return to a low heat (or better still to a double-boiler) to thicken the mixture slightly, though it should still remain creamy. Continue stirring all the time with the whisk

Adjust the seasoning to taste.

Put the scallops into the bottom of 4 small buttered molds and then fill with the mixture.

Place in an oven (260°F) and cook in a double-boiler for 30 minutes.

Before serving, put the reserved third of the original mixture in a double-boiler. Add the last egg yolk and gently thicken the sauce over a very low heat, stirring constantly with the whisk. Adjust seasoning to taste.

Turn out the ramekins onto warm plates and coat with the sauce.

Scallops with Grated Cheese

PREPARATION: 20 MINUTES
COOKING TIME: 20 MINUTES

SERVES: 4

INGREDIENTS:
8 large scallops (12 if medium-sized)
4 shells
3 chopped shallots
1 glass dry white wine
4 tablespoons sour cream
7 oz. grated Gruyère cheese
salt, freshly ground pepper, olive oil, nutmeg

Put a spoonful of olive oil in a casserole. Heat on a low flame. Add chopped shallots and cook until translucent. Do not brown.

Add the white wine. Salt and pepper to taste.

Separate the white of the scallops from their coral. Poach the whites for 1 minutes and reserve.

Reduce the wine to a quarter of its original volume. Add the coral, sour cream and grated Gruyère then liquefy.

Arrange the scallops on the shells and cover with the creamy sauce. Add a pinch of nutmeg.

Place under the broiler and cook for no more than 4 to 5 minutes, to avoid overcooking the scallops.

Sweet Pepper Polka with Bacon

PREPARATION: 20 MINUTES
COOKING TIME: 20 MINUTES

SERVES: 4

INGREDIENTS:
2 red peppers
2 green peppers
2 yellow peppers
about 20 pitted black
    olives
juice of 1 lemon
4 cloves garlic - crushed
3 tablespoons chopped
    fresh parsley
9 slices bacon
    (preferably Pancetta)
4 tablespoons olive oil
salt, freshly ground
    pepper

Cut the sweet peppers into halves. Remove the pith and the seeds.

Place the halved peppers skin side up under the oven grill and cook until the skin starts to char and bubble. Allow to cool and then peel.

Cut the sweet peppers into strips and place in a salad bowl.

Take one half of the olives and finely chop. Cut the remainder into halves.

With a fork, lightly beat the crushed garlic, lemon juice, olive oil and parsley, salt and freshly ground pepper together. Pour the mixture over the sweet peppers.

Cook the bacon over a low heat until it is completely crunchy. Reserve and allow to cool on absorbent kitchen paper.

Put the dry, crunchy bacon in a mixer and grind to a coarse powder.

Sprinkle the powder over the sweet peppers and serve.

V

Tomatoes Stuffed with Cracked Wheat

PREPARATION: 15 MINUTES
COOKING TIME: 60 MINUTES

SERVES: 4

INGREDIENTS:
8 large tomatoes
4 oz. cracked wheat (Bulghur)
10 cloves garlic
16 pitted black olives
3 tablespoons chopped parsley
olive oil, salt, freshly ground pepper, cayenne pepper, ras-el-hanout

Ras-el-hanout is a North African mixture of spices containing cinnamon, nutmeg, dried ginger, cloves and various peppers pounded together.

Halve the tomatoes across their segments and hollow out with a spoon. Reserve the pulp in a salad bowl. Arrange the tomatoes on an oven tray and place in a warm oven (320°F) for 30 minutes. Reserve.

In a bowl, crush the tomato pulp. Add the crushed cloves of garlic, the puréed black olives, the chopped parsley, 3 tablespoons of olive oil and the unrefined semolina. Add salt, freshly ground pepper, cayenne pepper and a few pinches of the ras-el-hanout. Mix-in well with a spoon and allow to stand for at least an hour.

Fill the tomato halves with the mixture and put back in a warm oven (320°F).

Serve hot.

69

Soups

71

Andalousian Gaspacho

PREPARATION: 15 MINUTES
COOKING TIME: 40 MINUTES

SERVES: 5

INGREDIENTS:
1 large cucumber
1 zucchini
2½ lb. tomatoes
2 red peppers
2 chopped onions
5 cloves garlic - crushed
juice of 3 lemons
12 leaves fresh basil
5 tablespoons olive oil
salt, freshly ground
    pepper, cayenne

72

Gaspacho is always served cold, with the addition of ice cubes.

Top and tail the zucchini and halve lengthwise. Cook in a steamer for 30 minutes. Allow to cool.

Top and tail the cucumber and halve lengthwise. Remove the seeds.

Cover the tomatoes in boiling water for 30 seconds. Pour off water and peel away the split skins. Cut open and remove seeds.

Cut the peppers in half lengthwise, remove pith and seeds, place on a tray and put under the grill skin side up until the skin bubbles and chars slightly. Peel.

Liquify one half of the cucumber, the zucchini, half of the peppers, three-quarters of the tomatoes, the onions, garlic, olive oil and the lemon juice. Add salt, freshly ground pepper and cayenne. Liquify. If the mixture is too thick, thin with tomato juice. Place in the refrigerator for at least 4 hours.

Before serving, cut the rest of the cucumber, tomatoes and peppers into cubes and serve separately as an accompaniment to the gaspacho.

Cabbage Soup

PREPARATION: 5 MINUTES
COOKING TIME: 2 HOURS 15 MINUTES

SERVES: 6

INGREDIENTS:
1 large savoy cabbage
7 oz. smoked bacon
10 oz. cured ham - thickly sliced
7 oz. marbled bacon
4 small celeriac - diced
2 onions
freshly ground pepper

Fill a large heavy saucepan with 6½ pints of water. Put into it the ham, smoked bacon and marbled bacon.

Bring to the boil. Skim.

Remove any tired leaves from the cabbage. Remove the stem and cut the cabbage into four. Add to the stockpot, together with the diced celeriac and the peeled onions.

Season with pepper. Reduce the heat, cover and allow to cook for 2 hours.

Take out the meat and half of the vegetables, which will make up the main dish later.

Put the remainder (liquid and vegetables) into the blender to make the soup.

Serve very hot.

73

Chilled Cream of Cucumber Soup

PREPARATION: 10 MINUTES
NO COOKING

SERVES: 4

INGREDIENTS:
1 large cucumber
16 fl.oz. greek yogurt
3 oz. finely ground
    almonds
2 cloves garlic - crushed
3 tablespoons olive oil
7 fl.oz. whipping cream
salt, white pepper
parsley

Peel the cucumber. Cut along its length. Remove seeds and dice. Sprinkle with salt and drain for 10 minutes. Liquify in a blender or food processor.

In a large bowl, mix the cucumber purée, yogurt, ground almonds, crushed garlic, olive oil and whipping cream. Season with salt and pepper.

Chill in a refrigerator for at least 6 hours.

Serve on chilled plates and sprinkle with freshly chopped parsley.

74

Cream of Garlic Soup

PREPARATION: 20 MINUTES
COOKING TIME: 30 MINUTES

SERVES: 4

INGREDIENTS:
4 handsome garlic heads (of approximately 20 cloves)
2 zucchinis
14 fl.oz. table cream
salt, freshly ground pepper, cayenne
2 tablespoons olive oil
2 tablespoons freshly chopped parsley

Peel the garlic cloves and place on one level of the steamer.

Halve the zucchinis, remove the seeds and cut into 1½ in. cubes. Place on the other level of the steamer.

Cook for 20 minutes.

Put the garlic, zucchini, olive oil and table cream in the mixer, adding salt, freshly ground pepper and cayenne to taste. Liquefy.

Transfer to a pan and reheat gently, adding some milk if necessary, to thin the mixture.

Serve and sprinkle a little chopped parsley on each plate.

75

Cream of Leek Soup

PREPARATION: 15 MINUTES
COOKING TIME: 35 MINUTES

SERVES: 4

INGREDIENTS:
5 or 6 good sized leeks
7 fl.oz. soy cream
1½ chicken bouillon
  cubes
1 bunch of parsley
salt and white pepper

Clean the leeks thoroughly and remove most of the green of the leaves.

Cut into pieces 1½ in. long.

Cook in a steamer for 30 minutes.

In the meantime, prepare 1½ pints of chicken stock.

Liquefy the leeks with some of the stock.

Pour the leek purée into the pan containing the stock and add the soy cream. Salt and pepper to taste.

Serve hot and decorate with chopped parsley.

76

Cream of Mussel Soup

PREPARATION: 15 MINUTES
COOKING TIME: 20 MINUTES

SERVES: 4

INGREDIENTS:
2¼ lb. mussels in their shells
4 large shallots
7 fl.oz. dry white wine
juice of 1 lemon
6 oz. sour cream
olive oil
3 tablespoons chopped fresh parsley
salt, freshly ground pepper

Clean the mussels in several changes of water and remove the beards.

Discard mussels with broken shells.

Chop the shallots very finely. Brown gently in some olive oil in a large saucepan.

Moisten with the white wine. Season with salt and pepper. Leave to cook for 1 to 2 minutes.

Add the mussels. Cover and cook over a high heat for 5 minutes until the shells have opened.

Take the mussels out of the pot with a slotted spoon and remove from their shells.

Reserve and keep warm.

Add lemon juice and parsley to the cooking juices. Add ground pepper and then the cream. Simmer for 3 minutes.

Return the mussels to the liquid, simmer for a further 2 minutes and serve.

77

Cream of Shrimp Soup

PREPARATION: 25 MINUTES
COOKING TIME: 30 MINUTES

SERVES: 4/5

INGREDIENTS:
2 pints prawns
2 onions - finely sliced
2 stalks of celery
9 fl.oz. white wine
1 sprig of thyme
1 bay leaf
5 oz. sour cream
2 egg yolks
olive oil

Chop the celery stalks into small pieces.

Shell the prawns.

In a covered pan, heat 3 tablespoons of olive oil over a medium heat. Add the onions, celery, thyme and bay leaf. Brown lightly, stirring constantly for 3 to 4 minutes.

Add the prawns, and continue cooking for 3 minutes.

Pour in the wine, cover and cook for a further 10 minutes, over a low heat.

Remove the thyme and bay leaf. Put the rest in a mixer and blend. Return to the pan, adding 1¼ pints of water. Add freshly ground pepper and salt to taste.

Cook over a low heat for about 5 minutes.

Beat the egg yolks and the sour cream together in a bowl. Pour the soup gradually into the egg-cream mixture, beating continuously.

Serve in warm bowls.

Cream of Soy with Shallots

PREPARATION: 15 MINUTES
COOKING TIME: 20 MINUTES

SERVES: 4

INGREDIENTS:
10 shallots
10 fl.oz. dry white wine
14 fl.oz. soy cream
olive oil
fine sea salt
freshly ground pepper,
    cayenne
Herbs de Provence

Cut the shallots into small pieces and put into the blender with 3 tablespoons of olive oil to make a purée.

In a saucepan, heat the purée over a very low flame for 5 to 6 minutes, making sure it does not catch or caramelize.

Add the white wine and bring to a boil. Add 1 teaspoon of Herbs de Provence and allow to simmer gently for 5 minutes. Reserve over a low heat.

Add the soy cream, 1 teaspoon of sea salt and 2 pinches of cayenne pepper. Heat for 4 to 5 minutes over a low flame (soy cream can coagulate over a heat that is too high).

Serve hot in soup plates.

Dandelion Soup

PREPARATION: 15 MINUTES
COOKING TIME: 30 MINUTES

SERVES: 4

INGREDIENTS:
13 oz. young dandelion
  leaves
3 small celeriac - diced
2 onions
6 cloves garlic
1 tablespoons goose fat
2 tablespoons olive oil
salt, freshly ground
  pepper

Wash the dandelion leaves.

Chop the garlic and onion. In a covered saucepan, brown in the olive oil.

Add 1½ pints of water to the saucepan, adding also the dandelion leaves and coarsely diced celeriac. Season with salt, pepper and cook on a low heat for 20 minutes.

Pour into a mixer. Add goose fat and liquefy.

Return blended mixture to the saucepan. Adjust seasoning and cook for a further 5 minutes before serving.

Pistou Soup

PREPARATION: 30 MINUTES
COOKING TIME: 1 HOUR 10 MINUTES

SERVES: 5/6

INGREDIENTS:
2¼ lb. fresh broad beans
(or dried beans that
have been soaked
overnight)
5 oz. sweet) peas
10 oz. zucchinis
4 very ripe tomatoes
2 large onions
4 gloves garlic
1 tablespoon chopped
fresh basil
salt, freshly ground
pepper
5 oz. grated Parmesan of
Emmental cheese

FOR THE PISTOU:
4 very ripe tomatoes
4 tablespoons chopped
fresh basil
5 cloves garlic
3 fl.oz. olive oil

String and wash the sugar peas.

Cut the zucchinis into halves and then into slices of about 1 inch thick.

Cut the onions into thin slices and crush the cloves of garlic.

Cover the tomatoes with boiling water for 30 seconds. Remove the tomatoes. Peel and cut them into halves, and remove the seeds. Chop the flesh coarsely.

Put the beans, zucchinis, onions, garlic, tomatoes, sweet peas and basil into a large pan. Cover with water. Sprinkle with salt.

Bring to a boil and leave to cook over a low heat for one hour.

In the meantime, prepare the pistou:

Cover the tomatoes with boiling water, peel, halve, remove the seeds, chop and allow to drain.

Quarter the cloves of garlic.

Liquefy the tomatoes, garlic, basil and olive oil. Season with salt and pepper.

When the soup is ready, add the pistou. Stir, sprinkle the grated cheese on top, and serve.

Sauerkraut Soup

PREPARATION: 15 MINUTES
COOKING TIME: 60 MINUTES

SERVES: 4

INGREDIENTS:
10 oz. sauerkraut
1½ pint meat stock
2 chopped onions
1 bay leaf
7 fl.oz. light cream
olive oil
salt, freshly ground
pepper

82

Drain the sauerkraut and then blanch for 10 minutes in boiling water.

In a heavy saucepan, brown the chopped onions in the olive oil over a gentle heat.

Add the sauerkraut and cook until it has colored slightly. Add a little stock to moisten and then liquefy in a blender or food processor.

Return the purée to the stockpot and add the rest of the stock and the bay leaf. Allow to cook for a further 40 minutes.

Add the light cream during the last 5 minutes of the cooking. Adjust the seasoning and serve.

Smooth Cucumber Soup with Greek Yogurt

PREPARATION: 20 MINUTES
NO COOKING

SERVES: 4

INGREDIENTS:
2 cucumbers
2 tomatoes
16 fl.oz. Greek yogurt
juice of 2 lemons
1 tablespoon olive oil
5 leaves fresh mint
1 bunch parsley
salt, freshly ground
    pepper

Put tomatoes into boiling water and leave for 30 seconds. Quarter, then peel and remove the seeds. Dice finely and reserve.

Peel the cucumber and remove the seeds. Put in a mixer together with the yogurt, lemon juice, mint, olive oil, salt and pepper. Liquefy.

Transfer the liquid to the refrigerator and chill for at least 5 hours.

Serve very cold, decorated with the diced tomatoes and freshly chopped parsley.

83

Smooth Mushroom Soup with Soy Cream

PREPARATION: 30 MINUTES
COOKING TIME: 1 HOUR 5 MINUTES

SERVES: 4

INGREDIENTS:
1 lb. button mushrooms
2 shallots - thinly sliced
1 onion - thinly sliced
7 fl.oz. soy cream
1 chicken bouillon cube
olive oil
salt, freshly ground
    pepper, curry
a large bunch of parsley

84

Clean the mushrooms. Cut in half and cook in 2 pints of salted water for 35 minutes.

Reserve the mushrooms and reduce the liquid for 10 minutes after having added the bouillon cube.

Heat the oil in a saucepan and cook the onion and shallots gently until translucent.

Moisten with the 9 fl.oz. of chicken stock. Reduce to simmering for 5 to 10 minutes.

Put the mushrooms in a mixer together with the soy cream and liquefy. Transfer to the saucepan. Warm through over a low heat for 4 to 5 minutes.

Thin if necessary, with the rest of the chicken stock. Season with salt and pepper. Add a pinch of curry.

Serve hot into plates and sprinkle with chopped parsley.

Sorrel Soup

PREPARATION: 15 MINUTES
COOKING TIME: 20 MINUTES

SERVES: 4

INGREDIENTS:
10 oz. sorrel
5 fl.oz. dry white wine
2 shallots - finely
    chopped
9 fl.oz. chicken stock
4 oz. sour cream
2 egg yolks
salt, freshly ground
    pepper
olive oil

Pour 1 tablespoon of olive oil into a heavy saucepan. Lightly brown the shallots over a low heat. Add the wine. Salt and pepper. Simmer and reduce by a third.

Wash the sorrel. Cut the leaves in half and add to the reduced wine. Cover and keep warm.

In another pan, bring the chicken stock to the boil.

In a metal bowl, mix the sour cream and the egg yolks together. Add the stock slowly and continue to stir the mixture with a whisk.

Pour the reduced wine and sorrel into the stock. Stir together and adjust seasoning to taste.

Keep the soup warm in a double-boiler until ready to serve.

85

Tomato Consommé

PREPARATION: 15 MINUTES
COOKING TIME: 25 MINUTES

SERVES: 4

INGREDIENTS:
2¼ lb. tomatoes
3 cloves of garlic - crushed
3 shallots - chopped
2 sprigs of basil
2 oregano tips
salt, freshly ground pepper

Heat a tablespoon of olive oil in a casserole and brown the garlic and shallots over a low heat.

Cover the tomatoes with boiling water and allow to stand for 30 seconds. Then peel and remove the seeds. Cut the flesh into pieces and place in the casserole. Season with salt.

Remove the leaves from the stems of basil and reserve. Chop the basil stems and add to the casserole with the oregano. Raise the temperature and allow to simmer for 10 minutes, partially covering with a lid to reduce spattering.

Liquefy. Adjust salt to taste and add ground pepper and finely chopped basil leaves.

Reheat and serve.

Eggs

Eggs with Tapenade Stuffing

PREPARATION: 15 MINUTES
COOKING TIME: 10 MINUTES

SERVES: 4

INGREDIENTS:
6 eggs
1 small jar (1½ oz.)
   Tapenade, or home
   made Tapenade
1 tablespoon olive oil
lettuce leaves
bunch of parsley

Boil the eggs for 10 minutes until hard. Cool in cold water.

Remove the shell and cut lengthwise into halves. Scoop out the yolk with a small spoon and place the whites on a serving dish covered with lettuce leaves.

Crush the yolks with a fork and mix with the tapenade and olive oil, to make a smooth paste.

Using the small spoon, fill the whites with the mixture.

Sprinkle freshly chopped parsley over the eggs and serve.

88

Lightly Fried Eggs and Cured Ham

PREPARATION: 2 MINUTES
COOKING TIME: 40 MINUTES

SERVES: 4

INGREDIENTS:
8 large fresh farm eggs
8 slices cured ham, cut finely
goose fat
salt, freshly ground pepper

In individual pans, cook the eggs in pairs in the goose fat. Do this over a low heat, to ensure the eggs do not crisp and brown at the edges.

Season with sea salt and freshly ground pepper.

Arrange the ham slices on individual plates and serve the eggs on top.

Mimosa Eggs with Tuna

PREPARATION: 15 MINUTES
COOKING TIME: 10 MINUTES

SERVES: 4

INGREDIENTS:
6 eggs
3½ oz. classic
  mayonnaise -
  preferably homemade
3½ oz. Italian tuna in
  brine
1 tablespoon chopped
  parsley
8 anchovy fillets
12 olives

90

Boil the eggs for 10 minutes until hard. Cool in cold water.

Remove the shell and cut lengthwise into halves. Scoop out the yolk with a small spoon.

Crush the yolks with a fork to make the mimosa. Reserve.

Drain the tuna and break up with a fork. Mix with the mayonnaise, a quarter of the mimosa and the chopped parsley.

With a small spoon, fill the egg whites.

Put 3 filled egg halves on each plate. Sprinkle with the rest of the mimosa. Decorate with the anchovies and olives.

Poached Eggs Provençale

PREPARATION: 10 MINUTES
COOKING TIME: 150 MINUTES

SERVES: 4

INGREDIENTS:
8 very fresh eggs
1 lb. puréed tomatoes
4 cloves garlic
4 tablespoons olive oil
1 tablespoon Herbs de Provence
1 tablespoon chopped fresh basil
salt, freshly ground pepper, wine vinegar

The eggs must be very fresh. Otherwise, when put in the water they will not remain compact.

In a non-stick pan, cook the puréed tomatoes, crushed cloves of garlic, Herbs de Provence and basil over a low heat.

Season with salt and pepper.

Stir constantly with a wooden spoon to prevent splashing. When the sauce mixture is hot, cover and allow to simmer on a gentle heat.

Boil 4 pints of water together with 2 tablespoons of wine vinegar and ¼ teaspoon of salt.

Break the eggs into a ladle and one by one lower carefully into the boiling water. Immediately reduce the heat and simmer for three and a half minutes. Remove the poached eggs with a slotted spoon and drain on a tea towel. Trim if desired, to improve their appearance.

Add olive oil to the tomato sauce and stir vigorously.

Serve the eggs on hot plates and coat with the tomato sauce.

Ramekin Eggs with Tarragon

PREPARATION: 15 MINUTES
COOKING TIME: 18 MINUTES

SERVES: 4

INGREDIENTS:
8 large eggs (very fresh)
3 very thin slices cured ham
8 tablespoons sour cream
1 bunch of fresh tarragon

Strip the tarragon and chop finely.

Chop the ham finely.

Butter the ramekins, which should be big enough to accommodate 2 eggs each.

Put half the tarragon in the ramekins. Break the eggs over the top.

In a bowl, mix the sour cream, the ham, and the rest of the tarragon. Season with salt and pepper.

Pour mixture over the eggs in each ramekin.

Cook in a double-boiler for 8 to 10 minutes in a very cool pre-heated oven (260°F).

Scrambled Eggs with Prawns

PREPARATION: 20 MINUTES
COOKING TIME: 20 MINUTES

SERVES: 4

INGREDIENTS:
10 oz. uncooked prawns
6 eggs
1 shallot - chopped
9 fl.oz. dry white wine
2 tablespoons chopped dill
salt, freshly ground pepper
1 tablespoon olive oil

Cook the prawns for about 2 minutes in bouillon stock and then shell.

In a frying pan, lightly brown the chopped shallot in the olive oil for about 3 minutes.

Add the white wine. Season with salt and pepper. Reduce by a third. Add the prawns, mix, reserve and keep warm.

Whisk the eggs in a metal bowl. Season with salt and pepper. Cook in a double-boiler, whisking constantly.

Turn out the scrambled eggs onto a warm serving dish and decorate with the prawn sauce.

Sprinkle with the dill and serve.

93

Scrambled Eggs with Red Peppers

PREPARATION: 15 MINUTES
COOKING TIME: 25 MINUTES

SERVES: 4

INGREDIENTS:
10 eggs
2 red peppers
Herbs de Provence
olive oil
salt, freshly ground
    pepper, mild paprika

Slice the red peppers lengthwise in two. Remove the pith and seeds.

Place the pepper halves under the broiler, skin side up until slightly charred and bubbled.

Allow to cool and then peel.

Purée the flesh in a mixer.

In a bowl, beat the eggs with the salt, pepper and paprika. Add the pepper purée and mix well.

Cook over a low heat in a pan containing olive oil - or better still, in a double-boiler - continuing to stir all the time.

Dust slightly with the Herbs de Provence and decorate with a drizzle of olive oil.

Serve.

94

Scrambled Eggs with Sorrel

PREPARATION: 15 MINUTES
COOKING TIME: 15 MINUTES

SERVES: 4

INGREDIENTS:
12 oz. sorrel
7 fl.oz. light cream
4 eggs
2 tablespoons sour cream
salt, freshly ground
    pepper
olive oil

If sorrel is difficult to obtain, substitute with spinach.

Wash the sorrel and dry well.

Put olive oil in a deep frying pan or wok. Add the leaves and soften over a very low heat. Add the sour cream. Season with salt and pepper.

Reserve and keep warm.

Beat the cream until stiff.

Break the eggs in a large metal bowl. Season with salt and pepper. Beat until frothy.

Put the bowl in a double-boiler and cook, beating constantly.

When the mixture is on the point of setting, gradually fold in the light cream.

Continue cooking.

Lay the sorrel leaves on the plates and pour the eggs over the top.

95

Scrambled Eggs with Truffle Crumbs

PREPARATION: 15 MINUTES
COOKING TIME: 15 MINUTES

SERVES: 4

INGREDIENTS:
10 eggs
¾ oz. tinned truffle
    crumbs
2½ oz. goose fat
salt, freshly ground
    pepper

Separate yolks from whites. Put the whites into a large metal bowl and whisk into stiff peaks. Lightly beat the yolks and blend with the whites. Season with salt and pepper.

Add the truffle crumbs with their juice.

Put the bowl into a double-boiler and start cooking, stirring constantly with the whisk and gradually adding the goose fat.

When the mixture has set but is still slightly creamy, pour onto a serving dish and serve immediately.

96

Tarragon Eggs in Aspic

PREPARATION: 15 MINUTES
COOKING TIME: 20 MINUTES

SERVES: 4

INGREDIENTS:
8 very fresh eggs
2 slices cooked ham
1 packet aspic powder
16 leaves of tarragon
3 fl.oz. white wine
    vinegar
salt, freshly ground
    pepper

The eggs must be very fresh. Otherwise, when put in the water they will not remain compact.

In a large casserole, bring 1 pint of water to a boil.

Add the white wine vinegar, salt and pepper.

Break each egg into a ladle and lower gently into the boiling water to release the egg. Immediately reduce the heat and simmer. Poach the eggs for 3 minutes. Remove with a slotted spoon and drain on a tea towel. Allow to cool.

Prepare the instant aspic as instructed on the packet. Allow to cool slightly and pour ¼ in. of the liquid into the bottom of 8 small molds (or ramekins).

Place in the freezer for a few minutes so that the aspic can set more quickly.

Place a poached egg in each mold. Then add two leaves of tarragon and a piece of ham to fit the diameter of the mold. Cover with the remaining aspic.

Allow to stand in the refrigerator for 3 hours and then turn out by first dipping the bottom of the molds into hot water for a few seconds.

Put back in the refrigerator until ready to serve. Serve on a bed of lettuce.

97

Tortilla Montignac

PREPARATION: 20 MINUTES
COOKING TIME: 15 MINUTES

SERVES: 4

INGREDIENTS:
8 eggs
2 onions - finely
    chopped
4 cloves garlic - finely
    chopped
3 zucchinis finely sliced
3 tablespoons freshly
    chopped parsley
9 oz. tomatoes - diced
    and well drained
7 oz. Mozzarella
Herbs de Provence
olive oil
salt, freshly ground
    pepper, cayenne

In a very large frying pan, lightly brown the onion and garlic in the olive oil over a low heat. Add the zucchinis and possibly some more olive oil to the pan. Sauté, taking care that the onion and the garlic do not carmelize.

Beat the eggs and season with salt, pepper and cayenne, adding the chopped parsley.

Pour the eggs into the pan and return to a gentle heat, without stirring.

While the eggs are cooking, sprinkle the tomato cubes evenly over the mixture in the pan.

Preheat the oven broiler to 500°F.

When the tortilla is nearly cooked, sprinkle with Herbs de Provence and spread the finely sliced mozzarella evenly over the top.

Complete the cooking by placing the pan with the tortilla about 6 in. under the broiler.

Drizzle chili flavored olive oil over the top and serve.

Tuna Omelette

PREPARATION: 15 MINUTES
COOKING TIME: 10 MINUTES

SERVES: 4

INGREDIENTS:
8 eggs
7 oz. tuna in brine
7 fl.oz. light cream
2 tablespoons freshly
  chopped parsley
olive oil

Drain the tuna and mash finely with a fork.

Separate the egg whites and the yolks into different bowls.

Whisk the whites into stiff peaks.

Whisk the yolks together with the light cream. Add the tuna and the parsley.

Fold the mixture delicately into the egg whites.

Heat a tablespoon of olive oil in a large pan. Pour the mixture and cook at normal temperature.

Serve while still slightly moist.

99

Meat

101

Beef Casserole

PREPARATION: 15 MINUTES
COOKING TIME: 2 HOURS 50 MINUTES

SERVES: 5

INGREDIENTS:

3¼ lb. chuck steak cut into 2 in. cubes

7 oz. bacon cubes

12 oz. mushrooms - sliced

9 fl.oz. dry red wine

10 pickling onions or shallots

9 fl.oz. beef stock

1 bouquet garni

1 sprig parsley

goose fat

Recommended side dishes: Celeriac purée
Onion purée

Fry the bacon cubes on a low heat. Add the whole onions until they are lightly browned.

Remove and reserve.

In a large casserole heat 3 tablespoons of goose fat. Add the cubes of meat and when they are lightly browned, add the stock.

Add the bacon cubes and onions to the contents of the casserole. Pour in the red wine. Season with salt, pepper, and add the bouquet garni. Cover and cook on a low heat for at least 2 hours.

In a separate pan, cover the sliced mushrooms with a ladle of stock and cook for 15 minutes. Liquefy half the mushrooms together with some of the cooking fluid. Add to the large casserole, with the rest of the mushrooms.

Allow to cook for 30 minutes with no lid. Remove the bouquet garni, adjust the seasoning, serve in a deep plate and sprinkle with parsley.

102

Beef Casserole Provençale

PREPARATION: 15 MINUTES
COOKING TIME: 1 HOUR 30 MINUTES

SERVES: 5

INGREDIENTS:
2¼ lb. braising steak or chuck steak cut into cubes
5 oz. marbled bacon - diced
4 finely sliced onions
10 fl.oz. red wine
1 bouquet garni
20 green olives - stones removed
20 black olives - stones removed
3 oz. canned mushrooms
olive oil, salt, freshly ground pepper

Recommended side dishes: Celeriac purée
Sweet pepper purée

In a casserole, heat 2 tablespoons of olive oil. On a low heat fry the diced bacon and then the sliced onions.

Add the pieces of meat and brown all over. Season with salt and pepper.

Add the bouquet garni and the wine. Cover and allow to simmer for 45 minutes.

Strain the mushrooms and transfer to a blender. Add a tablespoon of the cooking fluid and purée.

Add the mushroom purée and olives to casserole. Cover and continue cooking over a low heat for 30 minutes. Remove the cover and cook for a further 30 minutes.

Serve hot after removing the bouquet garni.

103

Blanquette of Veal Montignac

PREPARATION: 30MINUTES
COOKING TIME: 1 HOUR 15 MINUTES

SERVES: 5

INGREDIENTS:
3¼ lb. shoulder of veal,
   with no fat or bone,
   cut into 1 in. cubes
2¼ lb. button mushrooms
8 leeks
3 onions
4 cloves garlic
1 bouquet garni
3 pints veal stock
14 fl.oz. light cream
2 egg yolks
juice of 2 lemons
3 tablespoons chopped
   fresh parsley
goose fat

104

As this dish contains a lot of vegetables, it should be served as a dish on its own.

Prepare the vegetables: wash and cut the leeks into rings, clean the mushrooms and slice. Slice the onions and garlic thinly.

Put goose fat into a pan with a lid and brown the pieces of meat over a gentle heat. Season with salt and pepper. Put all the vegetables on top of the meat as well as the bouquet garni.

Pour the stock over the top and bring to the boil. Then turn down the heat, cover and allow to cook gently for an hour and a quarter.

Using a slotted spoon, remove half of the mushrooms, leeks, and onions. Drain them well and put them into a blender to make a purée.

Transfer the purée into a casserole together with the light cream. Add 2 egg yolks and stir continuously with the whisk for several minutes. When the cream begins to thicken, remove from the heat and continue to stir for 1 or 2 minutes.

Take the pan with the meat and pour off three quarters of the stock, to leave the meat, vegetables and a small amount of cooking liquid. Remove the bouquet garni.

Pour the sauce over the top and mix well, leaving the blanquette to stand in a warm place to ensure it maintains its temperature without cooking further.

Serve on warm plates.

Calf's Liver with Basil

PREPARATION: 5 MINUTES
COOKING TIME: 10 MINUTES

SERVES: 4

INGREDIENTS:
4 slices calf's liver each
  slice about 6 oz.
20 leaves basil - chopped
4 cloves garlic - crushed
olive oil
salt, freshly ground
  pepper

Recommended side dishes according to season:
  Ratatouille
  Braised chicory
  Provençale tomatoes

Mix the crushed garlic, the chopped basil, and 3 dessert spoons of olive oil.

Put this mixture in a big frying pan and cook for 3 minutes on a very gentle heat.

Add the slices of veal and cook on each side over a medium heat for 3 minutes.

Serve on a warm plate.

105

Calf's Liver with Onions

PREPARATION: 15 MINUTES
COOKING TIME: 15 MINUTES

SERVES: 4

INGREDIENTS:
4 slices calf's liver
   (6 oz. each)
10 large onions
olive oil
goose fat
4 oz. light cream
1 tablespoon balsamic
   vinegar
salt, freshly ground
   pepper

Slice the onions.

Heat a small amount of olive oil in a large non-stick frying pan. Add the onions. Then season with salt and pepper. Do not brown the onions, but cook until almost transparent.

In another frying pan, cook the slices of liver in the goose fat. Season with salt and pepper, reserve and keep warm.

De-glaze the second frying pan with the balsamic vinegar and the light cream. Add the cooked onions and stir well into the mixture.

Serve on warm plates, coating the liver with the onion sauce.

English Leg of Lamb - French Style

PREPARATION: 15 MINUTES
COOKING TIME: 60 MINUTES

SERVES: 5

INGREDIENTS:
3¼ lb. leg of lamb
2 bunches mint
1 tablespoon fructose
1 glass cider vinegar
goose fat
salt, freshly ground pepper, cayenne

Recommended side dishes: Broccoli
French beans

Grease the roasting pan with goose fat.

Cover the bottom of the pan with mint leaves.

Brush the leg liberally with goose fat. Season with salt and pepper, and dust very lightly with cayenne all over.

Cook in the oven (375°F) for 1 hour 30 or 40 minutes, depending on how pink you prefer your lamb.

While the meat is cooking, chop finely two dozen leaves of mint.

Boil the cider vinegar in a pan together with the chopped mint for 2 minutes. Turn off the heat and allow to cool for 3 minutes. Add the fructose, stirring well to ensure that it dissolves completely. Liquefy and refrigerate. Remove the leg of lamb from the oven and carve in the pan, to ensure none of the juices are lost. Then arrange the meat on a hot serving dish.

De-glaze the cooking pan with a glass of boiling salted water and pour into a sauce boat.

Serve the meat with the mint sauce and the de-glazed cooking juices.

107

Sirloin Steaks Bordeaux Style

PREPARATION: 15 MINUTES
COOKING TIME: 30 MINUTES

SERVES: 4

INGREDIENTS:
2 Sirloin steaks weighing 16 oz. and 2 in. thick

7 fl.oz. red Bordeaux wine

3½ fl.oz. strong meat stock

3½ oz. canned button mushrooms

5 shallots - chopped

4 tablespoons goose fat

1 sprig thyme

2 bay leaves

1 bunch of chopped parsley

salt and freshly ground pepper

Recommended side dishes: Mushrooms with parsley French beans

In a casserole heat 2 tablespoons of goose fat. Fry the shallots lightly for 2 to 3 minutes. Add a little red wine to moisten and then add the thyme, bay leaves, and stock. Season with salt and pepper. Over a strong heat with the lid removed, reduce the liquid by half.

Drain the mushrooms, place in a blender with a little olive oil and reduce to a purée. Add this purée to the sauce in the casserole.

In a large frying pan, heat the rest of the goose fat. Add the steaks and sear on both sides. Season with salt and pepper, and cook until the meat is either rare, medium or well done, according to individual taste.

De-glaze the frying pan with a little red wine. Add the de-glazing to the sauce.

Cut the steaks into 4 or 8 slices and arrange on a warm serving dish. Cover with the bordelaise sauce and serve.

Fillet of Veal Provençale

PREPARATION: 25 MINUTES
COOKING TIME: 1 HOUR 15 MINUTES

SERVES: 5

INGREDIENTS:
3¼lb. fillet of veal
2 large onions - sliced
4 large tomatoes
3 oz. tomato sauce
4 cloves garlic
3 oz. pitted green olives
1 glass white wine
7 oz. pickling onions or
   shallots
chopped parsley
olive oil
salt, pepper

Recommended side dishes: *Zucchini gratin*
Provençale tomatoes
Ratatouille

Cut the meat into cubes of about 2 in.

In a casserole, brown the veal on all sides in 3 tablespoons of olive oil. Season with salt and pepper. Reserve the veal on a separate dish.

In the same casserole, brown the onions over a low heat.

Pour boiling water over the tomatoes and leave for 30 seconds. Remove the skins and the seeds. Then dice the pulp and throw the pieces into the casserole together with the crushed garlic. Cook over a low heat for 5 minutes.

In a bowl, mix the tomato sauce with the glass of white wine and 1 tablespoon of olive oil. Then pour into the casserole.

Skin the small onions and cook in a pan of salted water for 30 seconds.

Return the veal to the casserole together with the onions and the olives. Stir well and cover, cooking over a very gentle heat for 30 minutes. Add a little wine if necessary while cooking, to prevent the meat from sticking to the bottom of the pan. Adjust seasoning.

Arrange on a warm serving dish, sprinkle with parsley and serve.

109

Goujons of Veal

PREPARATION: 20 MINUTES
COOKING TIME: 25 MINUTES

SERVES: 4

INGREDIENTS:
4 thick veal escalopes cut
    into ribbons (goujons)
7 oz. button mushrooms
3 onions - finely sliced
10 fl.oz. light cream
juice of 1 lemon
goose fat
salt, freshly ground
    pepper, nutmeg
olive oil

Recommended side dishes: Braised chicory
Extra thin French beans

Clean the mushrooms and slice. Brown over a low heat in a frying pan with olive oil. Season with salt and pepper. Throw away the water that has seeped out of the mushrooms and add a little olive oil.

Fry the onions in some olive oil over a low heat.

Melt 1 tablespoon of goose fat in a casserole. Over a low heat, brown the veal goujons, turning constantly. Season with salt, pepper, and add the lemon juice.

Add the button mushrooms and onions. Stir. Pour over the light cream and grate the nutmeg on top.

Stir together well and leave to cook on a very gentle heat with the lid off, for 2 or 3 minutes. Taste and adjust the seasoning.

Leg of Lamb with Rosemary

PREPARATION: 10 MINUTES
COOKING TIME: 30 MINUTES

SERVES: 4-5

INGREDIENTS:
4½ lb. leg of lamb
6 cloves garlic - crushed
1 large sprig rosemary
1 tablespoon of sea salt
freshly ground pepper
cayenne
goose fat

Recommended side dishes: Flageolet beans
French beans

In a large bowl, mix garlic purée, crumbled rosemary, salt, 2 tablespoons of softened goose fat, and 3 large pinches of cayenne.

Rub the mixture well into the leg of lamb. Put into a roasting pan with the fatty side up and roast (375°F) for 1 hour 50 minutes.

Melt 3 tablespoons of goose fat in 4 fl.oz. of boiling water, basting the leg every 15 minutes.

111

Mutton Fillet Provençale

PREPARATION: 15 MINUTES
COOKING TIME: 30 MINUTES

SERVES: 5

INGREDIENTS:
2¼ lb. mutton fillet or
   saddle - boned (If
   mutton is unavailable,
   substitute with lamb)
2 onions - finely sliced
2 cloves garlic - crushed
7 fl.oz. beef stock
7 oz. tomato sauce
olive oil
Herbs de Provence
salt, freshly ground
   pepper

Recommended side dishes: Ratatouille
Haricot beans

Cut the meat into 1 in. cubes.

Pour 2 tablespoons of olive oil into a casserole. Add onions and brown over a low heat. Then brown the cubes of mutton on all sides. Add the garlic and a couple of teaspoons of Herbs de Provence. Season with salt and pepper.

In a separate pan, slowly thin the tomato sauce with the hot stock. Add salt and pepper to taste.

Pour the tomato sauce into the casserole and mix well. Add 2 tablespoons of olive oil. With the lid on, continue cooking over a very low heat until the meat is just pink.

Serve hot.

Pork Chops with Cream of Mustard Sauce

PREPARATION: 10 MINUTES
COOKING TIME: 25 MINUTES

SERVES: 4

INGREDIENTS:

4 large pork chops (or 8 small chops)

3 oz. sour cream

3 tablespoons strong French mustard

1 tablespoon capers (preferably salted)

1 tablespoon goose fat

Recommended side dishes: Celeriac purée
French beans

In a bowl, mix the sour cream, mustard, and rinsed carpers.

Over a medium heat, melt the goose fat in a large frying pan and brown the chops for about 7 to 8 minutes on each side. Season with salt and pepper.

Pour the sauce over the chops. Cover the pan and allow to simmer for about 10 minutes.

Serve on warm plates.

Pork Shoulder Chops Provençale

PREPARATION: 15 MINUTES
COOKING TIME: 15 MINUTES

SERVES: 4

INGREDIENTS:
4 pork shoulder chops
4 shallots - sliced
7 fl.oz. white wine
3 or 4 tablespoons
 tomato sauce
olive oil, goose fat
Herbs de Provence
salt, freshly ground
 pepper

Recommended side dishes: *Zucchinis gratin*
Provençale tomatoes
Ratatouille

Heat 2 tablespoons of olive oil in a frying pan. Over a low heat brown the shallots. Moisten with a little white wine and cook for 5 minutes, stirring occasionally.

Thin the tomato sauce with the remainder of the wine. Add to the pan with a tablespoon of olive oil. Season with salt and pepper. Put aside and keep warm over a very, very low heat.

Sprinkle Herbs de Provence over the chops.

In a frying pan, heat a generous tablespoon of goose fat. Add the chops and cook over a low heat, browning first on one side and then on the other. Season with salt and pepper.

Arrange the chops on a warm plate and coat with the sauce.

Rack of Lamb Provençale

PREPARATION: 25 MINUTES
COOKING TIME: 45 MINUTES

SERVES: 4

INGREDIENTS:
1 rack of lamb, weighing about 2¼ lb. (8 good-size chops)
4 fl.oz. dry white wine
5 fl.oz. sour cream
1 tablespoon cognac
5 cloves garlic - peeled
olive oil
Herbs de Provence
14 oz. button mushrooms
salt, freshly ground pepper, cayenne
1 tablespoon of chopped parsley

Cut 2 cloves of garlic into a total of 8 slices. Make deep gashes in the rack of lamb (between each chop) and insert the slivers of garlic.

Coat the cooking pan with olive oil.

Mix 4 tablespoons of olive oil together with salt, pepper, and a pinch of cayenne.

Place the rack of lamb in the tin and brush with the seasoned olive oil. Sprinkle with the Herbs the Provence and place in a very hot oven (500°F). Cook for 20 to 25 minutes.

In the meantime, clean the mushrooms and remove the stalks. Cut into slices - the stalks down their length.

Brown the mushrooms over a very gentle heat, in a pan with olive oil. Season with salt and pepper. After a few minutes, remove the cooking juices and water they have produced.

Crush the 3 remaining cloves of garlic and mix them with the parsley. Add them to the mushrooms in the olive oil. Continue cooking over a gentle heat for several minutes, stirring well.

Take the rack of lamb out of the oven and cut it up in the cooking pan. Reserve the chops and keep warm.

De-glaze the pan with the white wine and cognac that have already been heated. Add the sour cream and pour into a warm sauceboat.

Serve the rack on a warm plate surrounded with mushrooms.

115

Roast Pork with Curry

PREPARATION: 15 MINUTES
COOKING TIME: 1 HOUR 15 MINUTES

SERVES: 4

INGREDIENTS:
4 lb. pork fillet
4 cloves garlic - skinned
3 tablespoons goose fat
7 fl.oz. light cream
curry
salt, freshly ground
    pepper

Recommended side dishes: Brussels sprouts
Broccoli
French beans

With a sharp pointed knife, make 4 deep cuts in the meat. Push the cloves of garlic deep into the flesh.

In a bowl, prepare a marinade with the melted goose fat. Season with salt, pepper, and 1 tablespoon of curry. Mix well.

Rub the mixture well into the meat.

Place the meat in a tin and pour around the meat the rest of the marinade together with ½ glass of water. Roast in the oven (450°F) for 1 hour 15 minutes.

Before serving, de-glaze the pan with the light cream.

116

Roast Veal with Olives

PREPARATION: 20 MINUTES
COOKING TIME: 1 HOUR 45 MINUTES

SERVES: 4-5

INGREDIENTS:
joint veal weighing
about 2½ lb.
4 oz. marbled bacon -
diced
7 oz. black olives -
stones removed
7 oz. green olives -
stones removed
5 fl.oz. white wine
salt, freshly ground
pepper, thyme

In a casserole fry the diced marbled bacon over a gentle heat. Add the veal and brown lightly all over. Season with salt and pepper, and sprinkle with a few pinches of thyme. Cover and cook over a very gentle heat.

Combine 1 tablespoon of olive oil with 3 oz green olives and 3 oz. black olives in a blender and reduce to a purée. Pour into the casserole and stir in the wine.

Cook over a very gentle heat for 1 hour, turning the meat from time to time.

Add the rest of the olives and allow to cook for a further 20 to 30 minutes, always over a low heat.

117

Take the roast out of the casserole. Slice and arrange on a warm dish and garnish with the olives.

Pour off the juices and set aside. Deglaze the residue on the bottom of the casserole with a little boiling water. Add the juices and stir.

Pour into a sauceboat and serve.

Rolled Escalopes with Ham Provence Style

PREPARATION: 20 MINUTES
COOKING TIME: 20 MINUTES

SERVES: 4

INGREDIENTS:
8 thin slices pork or veal
8 thin slices cured ham
3 tablespoons tomato
   paste
4 oz. shallots - chopped
3 cloves garlic - chopped
2 fl.oz. brandy
thyme
goose fat, olive oil
salt, freshly ground
   pepper

Recommended side dishes: *Eggplants with olive oil*
                                          Zucchinis gratin
                                          Sweet Peas

Sprinkle the thyme on one side of each escalope. Having first removed the rind and the fat, lay a slice of ham on top of each escalope. Roll and secure with string.

In a casserole heat 1 tablespoon of goose fat, brown the rolls of meat until golden.

At the same time, in a frying pan with a little olive oil, brown the sliced shallots and garlic over a gentle heat.

In a bowl, add 4 fl.oz. of water and a tablespoon of olive oil to the tomato paste. Season with salt and pepper.

Put the tomato paste, shallots, and garlic in the casserole. Stir and cook over a gentle heat for 2 or 3 minutes.

Note:

This dish can be kept hot and allowed to stand for a good quarter of an hour before serving.

118

Spare Rib of Pork Andalousia

PREPARATION: 15 MINUTES
COOKING TIME: 1 HOUR 15 MINUTES

SERVES: 4

INGREDIENTS:

1¾ lb. boned spare rib of pork

4 oz. marbled bacon - diced

1¾ lb. celeriac - peeled and washed

4 oz. black olives - stones removed

4 oz. green olives - stones removed

3 to 4 tablespoons tomato sauce

1 glass of port

salt, freshly ground pepper

olive oil

In a casserole heat some olive oil and fry the cubes of marbled bacon over a gentle heat.

Cut the celeriac into 1 inch cubes. Blanch for 3 minutes in salted boiling water. Drain well.

Cut the pork into pieces. Lightly brown over a low heat in the casserole for about 10 minutes, in the bacon fat. Season with salt, pepper, then add the celeriac, olives, and the tomato sauce. Pour over the pork and stir.

Cover the casserole and cook on a low heat for 1 hour.

119

Tournedos Provençale

PREPARATION: 15 MINUTES
COOKING TIME: 40 MINUTES

SERVES: 4

INGREDIENTS:
4 filet mignons cut from the fillet, about 8 oz. each
6 large ripe tomatoes
2 onions - sliced
3 red peppers
3 cloves garlic - finely sliced
olive oil, goose fat
salt, freshly ground pepper
Herbs de Provence

Cut the red peppers in half down their length. Remove the stalk and the seeds. Place under the broiler skin-side up. When the skin has bubbled and is slightly charred, put them on one side to cool.

Remove the skin and cut into strips about ½ in. thick.

Plunge the tomatoes into boiling water for about 30 seconds. Skin, remove the seeds, and cut into small cubes.

In a large frying pan heat 2 or 3 tablespoons of olive oil over a low heat. Brown the onions, stirring frequently. Add the garlic, diced tomatoes, and strips of red pepper.

Season with salt and pepper, and sprinkle a few Herbs de Provence sparingly over the top. Leave to cook over a gentle heat for 20 minutes.

In another frying pan, melt a lump of goose fat and brown the filet mignons (tournedos) 2 or 3 minutes each side. Season with salt and pepper.

Pour the tomato sauce over the meat and continue cooking for 2 minutes.

Serve hot.

Tournedos with Olives

PREPARATION: 15 MINUTES
COOKING TIME: 25 MINUTES

SERVES: 4

INGREDIENTS:
4 filet mignons - 8 oz. each
4 large tomatoes
20 pitted black olives
4 tablespoons anchovy paste
olive oil
salt, freshly ground pepper
Herbs de Provence

Cut each of the tomatoes into three. Place in an ovenware dish and brush with olive oil on both sides. Season with salt, pepper, and sprinkle with Herbs de Provence.

Put under the broiler until they are slightly browned. Reserve and keep warm.

In a frying pan, fry the black olives in the olive oil. Add the tomatoes.

Brush the filet mignons (tournedos) with the anchovy paste. Heat some olive oil in a frying pan and cook the meat for 2 or 3 minutes on each side. Do not salt.

Serve the tournedos very hot with the tomatoes, olives and their cooking juices.

121

Veal Chops Provençale

PREPARATION: 15 MINUTES
COOKING TIME: 25 MINUTES

SERVES: 4

INGREDIENTS:

4 veal chops, with fat removed approximate weight 8 oz. each

2 onions - finely sliced

3 garlic cloves - crushed

2 tablespoons freshly chopped basil

1 tablespoon freshly chopped parsley

3 tablespoons tomato sauce

white wine

goose fat

olive oil

Herbs de Provence

salt, freshly ground pepper

In a casserole heat 2 tablespoons of olive oil. Brown the onions over a low heat and when cooked, add the crushed garlic.

Add the tomato paste thinned with a little white wine to make it smooth and creamy. Season with salt, pepper, and add the fresh basil. Reserve and keep warm.

Season the veal chops and dust them with the Herbs de Provence.

Melt 1 tablespoons of goose fat in a frying pan and fry the veal chops gently over a medium heat - 7 to 8 minutes each side. Remove to a serving dish and keep warm.

Pour away the fat from the cooking juices and de-glaze the pan with ½ glass of white wine. Add the tomato paste. Turn off the heat and add a tablespoon of olive oil.

Coat the veal chops with the sauce and sprinkle with parsley.

Veal Chops with Sorrel Fondue

PREPARATION: 15 MINUTES
COOKING TIME: 15 MINUTES

SERVES: 4

INGREDIENTS:
4 veal chops, with fat
    removed - approximate
    weight 8 oz. each
5 oz. finely chopped
    sorrel
juice of 1 lemon
goose fat
olive oil
salt, freshly ground
    pepper

In a large frying pan, melt 1 tablespoon of goose fat over a gentle heat.

Put in the veal chops and brown for 5 to 7 minutes on each side. Season with salt and pepper, then reserve.

While the chops are cooking, remove the stalks from the sorrel and wash well. Dry with a tea towel or kitchen paper.

Pour 2 tablespoons of olive oil into a casserole and add the finely chopped sorrel. Cook gently on a low heat, stirring with a wooden spoon for about 5 minutes. Salt and pepper lightly.

Remove and throw away the excess fat from the cooking juices of the veal. De-glaze the bottom of the frying pan with the lemon juice, add the sorrel fondue and then the chops. Mix well and continue cooking over a low heat for 1 or 2 minutes.

Arrange on a serving dish, drizzle olive oil over the top and serve.

123

Veal Escalope with Parma Cream

PREPARATION: 15 MINUTES
COOKING TIME: 35 MINUTES

SERVES: 4

INGREDIENTS:
4 escalopes weighing about 1¼ lb.
6 slices Parma ham
1 onion
5 fl.oz. sour cream
1 tablespoon olive oil
goose fat
salt, pepper, cayenne

Recommended side dishes: Extra thin French beans
Sweet Peas

In a non-stick frying pan, cook the slices of Parma ham over a low heat (1 to 2 minutes on each side), making sure they are in overall contact with the bottom of the pan.

Dry them in the oven (260°F) until completely stiff and brittle. Cut into pieces and reduce to a powder in the blender. Reserve.

Slice the onion finely and fry in a little olive oil over a low heat. Add the Parma ham powder and the sour cream. Season with salt, pepper, and a pinch of cayenne.

Salt and pepper the escalopes. Melt the goose fat in a frying pan and gently fry the escalopes.

To serve, arrange on a dish or serve on warmed plates and coat with the Parma Cream.

Veal with Paprika

PREPARATION: 15 MINUTES
COOKING TIME: 1 HOUR 10 MINUTES

SERVES: 4

INGREDIENTS:
2¼ lb. fillet of veal
6 large onions - sliced
7 fl.oz. sour cream
7 fl.oz. white wine
goose fat
olive oil
1 bouquet garni
mild paprika
hot paprika
salt, freshly ground
    pepper

*Recommended side dishes: Braised chicory
                          Cauliflower gratin*

In a frying pan, fry the onions in olive oil over a gentle heat.

Cut the meat into cubes 1½ in. Heat the goose fat in a casserole and brown the meat on all sides.

Put the onions in the casserole. Add the white wine, bouquet garni, 3 teaspoons of mild paprika, 1 teaspoon of hot paprika, salt, and pepper. Stir well, cover the casserole and cook over a gentle heat for at least one hour.

Remove the pieces of meat, arrange on a serving dish and keep warm. Discard the bouquet garni.

Transfer the rest to a blender and reduce to a creamy sauce.

Add the sour cream and mix well.

Pour the sauce over the top of the meat and serve immediately.

125

Poultry

127

Capon with Prunes and Cognac Sauce

PREPARATION: 30 MINUTES
COOKING TIME: 2 HOURS 45 MINUTES

SERVES: 6-8

INGREDIENTS:
1 large capon about 8 lb
6 slices bacon
9 oz. diced marbled bacon
2 onions - sliced
3 eggs
3 slices toasted wholemeal bread, preferably pain intégrale
1 tablespoon goose fat
14 fl.oz. light cream
30 pitted prunes
4 fl.oz. brandy
1 sprig tarragon
½ teaspoon Herbs de Provence
salt, freshly ground pepper, cayenne
olive oil
7 fl.oz. white wine

Fry the marbled bacon. When there is sufficient melted fat in the pan, add the onions and brown.

In a bowl, mix the diced bacon, onions 7 fl.oz. double cream, eggs, and crumbs made from the toasted bread. Season generously with salt, pepper, and cayenne. Add chopped tarragon, Herbs de Provence. Mix well with a fork or in the blender. Fill the capon with stuffing.

Using the point of a knife, raise the skin of the capon and slide in the bacon slices to cover the carcass. Melt the goose fat over a very, very low heat and then brush liberally over the capon.

Put the capon into a large pan and cook in the oven (400°F) for 2 hours and 15 minutes.

Gently simmer the prunes in the white wine for 15 minutes. Drain and arrange in the cooking pan around the capon about 20 minutes before cooking is completed.

Take the capon out of the oven. Pour off about three quarters of the fat in the pan. Add the brandy, and flambé.

Carve the capon in the pan to conserve the juices. Then de-glaze with the remaining 7 fl.oz. of light cream. Arrange the pieces of capon on a warm plate, surrounded by the prunes. Reheat the sauce and pour into the sauceboat. Serve immediately.

CHEESE AND ONION ROSTI WITH BACON. *Recipe on page 55.*

CHILLED CREAM OF CUCUMBER SOUP. *Recipe on page 74.*

PISTON SOUP. *Recipe on page 81.*

Duck with Olives. Recipe on page 146.

Leg of Lamb with Rosemary. Recipe on page 111.

CHICKEN WITH APPLES AND CIDER CREAM. *Recipe on page 138.*

Turkey Escalopes with Cream. Recipe on page 157.

Lemon Sole Cretan Style. Recipe on page 169.

FILLETS OF SOLE WITH SALMON. *Recipe on page 164.*

SCALLOPS WITH SHALLOTS AND CREAM OF SOYA. *Recipe on page 192.*

TUNA WITH GARLIC VINEGAR. *Recipe on page 184.*

TAGLIATELLE WITH PESTO. *Recipe on page 214.*

Broccoli Salad with Almonds. Recipe on page 223.

Red Bean Salad. Recipe on page 230.

FRESH ALMOND MOUSSE. Recipe on page 247.

CHOCOLATE TRUFFLES.   *Recipe on page 243.*

PEACHES WITH CHEESE AND RASPBERRIES.   *Recipe on page 252.*

Chicken Breasts in Creamy Garlic Sauce

PREPARATION: 20 MINUTES
COOKING TIME: 60 MINUTES

SERVES: 4

INGREDIENTS:
4 boneless chicken breasts
2 heads garlic
10 fl.oz. soy cream
goose fat
salt, freshly ground pepper
mild paprika
cayenne
1 bunch parsley

Recommended side dishes: Ratatouille
Provençale tomatoes

Break up the heads of garlic, peel the cloves and cook in a steamer for 30 minutes.

Place the chicken breasts in an ovenware dish and brush with goose fat. Season with salt, pepper, and sprinkle lightly with cayenne.

Put in the oven (375°F) for 20 to 25 minutes.

Liquefy the garlic cloves with the soy cream. Season with salt, pepper, and add the equivalent of ½ teaspoon of mild paprika.

Remove the chicken breasts from the oven and cut across the width into ½ in. thick slices. Rearrange in the cooking dish.

Coat with the garlic cream and leave in a lukewarm oven (200°F) for 10 to 15 minutes.

Sprinkle with chopped parsley and serve.

129

Chicken Breasts and Tarragon in a Bag

PREPARATION: 20 MINUTES
COOKING TIME: 15 MINUTES

SERVES: 4

INGREDIENTS:
4 boneless chicken breasts
2 tomatoes
½ bunch fresh tarragon
juice of 1 lemon
4 tablespoons olive oil
salt, freshly ground pepper, cayenne
1 teaspoon strong mustard

Cut the tomatoes into thick slices. Salt on both sides and leave to drain on absorbent kitchen paper.

Pre-heat the oven (500°F).

Prepare the tarragon, choosing the best leaves.

Cut each chicken breast into 5 or 6 pieces and arrange in a bag made from kitchen foil, together with a couple of slices of tomato and the tarragon leaves.

Sprinkle with 1 tablespoon of olive oil and the juice of a ¼ lemon. Season with salt and pepper, add a pinch of cayenne, and close the bag. Put in the oven to cook for 15 minutes.

When ready, open the bags, pour off the liquid. Mix the liquid with the mustard (Phase 2).

Serve the chicken in the bag and pour the sauce over the top.

Chicken Breasts with Curry Sauce

PREPARATION: 20 MINUTES
COOKING TIME: 35 MINUTES

SERVES: 5

INGREDIENTS:
5 boneless chicken
   breasts
3 large onions - sliced
1 lb. button mushrooms
10 fl.oz. table cream
goose fat
olive oil
3 teaspoons curry
   powder
salt, pepper, mild
   paprika
Herbs de Provence

Fry the onions in some olive oil.

Clean the mushrooms, slice and cook in a steamer for 20 minutes.

Cut the chicken breasts into slices 1 in. thick.

Stir fry the chicken over a low heat in a little goose fat. Season with salt, mild paprika, and pepper, and dust with Herbs de Provence.

Ensure the chicken is white and evenly cooked.

Add the onions and the mushrooms to the chicken, followed by the cream and the 3 teaspoons of curry powder. Stir well and cover, cooking on a very, very low heat for 5 minutes.

Adjust the seasoning, bearing in mind individual preferences as far as the spiciness of curry is concerned.

Chicken Breasts with Lime

PREPARATION: 15 MINUTES
COOKING TIME: 45 MINUTES

SERVES: 4

INGREDIENTS:
4 boneless chicken
   breasts
5 garlic cloves - crushed
3 limes
4 tablespoons olive oil
salt, freshly ground
   pepper, cayenne

Recommended side dishes: Extra fine French beans
                                  Broccoli

In a bowl, make a marinade of lime juice, olive oil, crushed garlic, salt, and pepper. Mix well.

Dust the chicken breasts lightly with cayenne and immerse in the marinade.

Refrigerate a few hours, turning from time to time.

Drain the chicken breasts and put them in a roasting pan. Place in a preheated oven (375°F) and cook for 30 minutes.

In the meantime, pour the marinade into a pan, bring to the boil and reduce to obtain a thick sauce.

Serve the chicken breasts coated with this sauce.

Chicken Breasts Provençale

PREPARATION: 10 MINUTES
COOKING TIME: 15 MINUTES

SERVES: 4

INGREDIENTS:
4 boneless chicken
  breasts
18 oz. fresh tomato
  sauce or 9 oz. tomato
  paste + 9 fl.oz. water
1 tablespoon Herbs de
  Provence
4 tablespoons olive oil
4 cloves garlic crushed
salt, pepper, cayenne

Recommended side dish: *Green salad*

Cut the chicken breasts into slices 1 in. thick. Salt and sprinkle with cayenne.

Cook in a steamer for 5 minutes.

Meanwhile, pour the tomato sauce into a casserole. Add the garlic, the Herbs de Provence, and the 4 tablespoons of olive oil. Salt and pepper. Stir and put bach on a very gentle heat.

Turn the chicken breasts (with pink centers) into the casserole. Stir well, cover, and cook over an extremely low heat for 5 minutes with the lid on. Adjust seasoning before serving.

Variation:

If desired, drizzle a little olive oil over the chicken when served.

This dish can be prepared in advance and gently re-heated with the lid on.

133

Chicken Casserole in Wine

PREPARATION: 30 MINUTES
COOKING TIME: 1 HOUR 10 MINUTES

SERVES: 4

INGREDIENTS:
1 large fresh chicken (or free-range chicken, if available)
2 onions - chopped
2 cloves garlic
4 oz. diced marbled bacon
14 oz. canned mushrooms
18 fl.oz. red wine with a high tannin content, like Corbières, Côtes du Rhône
2 tablespoons goose fat
salt, freshly ground pepper, cayenne

Recommended side dishes: Celeriac purée
Onion purée

Cut the chicken up into several pieces and remove most of the skin.

Melt the goose fat in a casserole. Lightly brown the onions and garlic over a gentle heat.

In the meantime, brown the diced marbled bacon in a non-stick pan until most of the fat has melted.

Fry the chicken pieces in the casserole until golden brown. Add the marbled bacon without the melted fat and add a little red wine.

Season with salt, pepper, and cayenne. Raise the temperature and bring to the boil.

Reduce the heat and simmer.

Drain the mushrooms. Put half in the blender with a little wine and make a purée. Add to the contents of the casserole, together with the rest of the mushrooms.

Stir and simmer for an hour. Adjust the seasoning. Allow to cool.

Slowly reheat the coq-au-vin and serve.

Chicken in a Salt Crust

PREPARATION: 10 MINUTES
COOKING TIME: 1 HOUR 40 MINUTES

SERVES: 4

INGREDIENTS:
1 fresh chicken weighing about 3 lb. (or free-range chicken, if available)
5 to 6 lb. coarse salt
10 fl.oz. whipping cream
1 chicken bouillon cube

Recommended side dishes: Braised chicory
Cauliflower gratin
Zucchinis gratin

In a cast iron stock-pot big enough to take the chicken with ease, lay a bed of salt 1 in. thick.

Lay the chicken on top and cover with salt, to a depth of ½ in.

Place in a pre-heated oven (350°F) and cook for 1 hour 30 minutes.

Crack the crust and take out the chicken when ready to serve and eat.

As there are no cooking juices, a sauce may be prepared by dissolving 1 cube of chicken bouillon in 10 fl.oz. of whipping cream. To ensure the cube dissolves properly, grate it into a powder with the blade of a serrated knife. Avoid overheating the cream.

135

Chicken Livers with Celeriac Purée

PREPARATION: 15 MINUTES
COOKING TIME: 1 HOUR 15 MINUTES

SERVES: 4

INGREDIENTS:
1¼ lb. chicken livers
1 celeriac
1 lemon, cut into quarters
10 fl.oz. light cream
2 tablespoons balsamic vinegar
goose fat
salt, freshly ground pepper, nutmeg
1 bunch chervil

Peel, wash, and dice the celeriac. Cook for at least 1 hour in salted boiling water containing the lemon quarters. Check with the point of a sharp knife to confirm when cooking is complete.

Drain and discard the lemon. Add the light cream.

Season with salt and pepper, and dust with grated nutmeg. Allow to simmer on a very low heat until the cream has been absorbed by the celeriac.

Transfer to the blender and make into a purée. Check the seasoning and reserve.

In a frying pan, melt the goose fat and gently brown the livers. Season with salt and pepper. Add a sprinkling of balsamic vinegar.

Arrange the livers on individual plates. Add the celeriac purée and decorate with the chervil.

136

Chicken Provençale

PREPARATION: 15 MINUTES
COOKING TIME: 40 MINUTES

SERVES: 4-5

INGREDIENTS:
1 fresh chicken weighing about 3 lb. (or free-range chicken, if available)

1 large onion - sliced

4 cloves garlic - sliced

9 fl.oz. chicken stock

3 tablespoons tomato sauce

olive oil

salt, freshly ground pepper, cayenne

Herbs de Provence

Recommended side dish: Ratatouille

Cut the chicken into 8 pieces and arrange in an oven dish with the skin facing up.

Brush with olive oil. Season with salt, pepper, and cayenne.

Cook under the broiler for about 30 minutes. The skin should crisp slowly without getting charred. To avoid charring the skin, be sure the meat is not too close to the broiler.

In a casserole, brown the onions and the garlic in the olive oil. Pour over the stock and add the purée. Stir well, seasoning with salt and pepper.

Coat the pieces of chicken with the tomato sauce and sprinkle with some Herbs de Provence. Place the chicken in the casserole and put in the oven (260°F) for 5 or 10 minutes.

Serve in the casserole or in a warm serving dish.

137

Chicken with Apples and Cider Cream

PREPARATION: 20 MINUTES
COOKING TIME: 1 HOUR 40 MINUTES

SERVES: 5

INGREDIENTS:

1 fresh young chicken
weighing about 3 lb.
(or free-range
chicken, if available)

2¼ lb. apples

7 fl.oz. dry cider

1 chicken bouillon cube

7 fl.oz. light cream

2 teaspoons cinnamon

goose fat

salt, freshly ground
pepper, cayenne

Brush the chicken with a tablespoon of goose fat. Season with salt, pepper, and cayenne and place in a pre-heated oven (450°F).

Peel the apples and cut into pieces. Cook in the frying pan with goose fat, stirring regularly. Season liberally with salt, pepper, and cinnamon. Reserve.

To make the Cream of Cider sauce, boil the cider in a pan and reduce by three quarters. Add the chicken bouillon cube and dissolve well, then add the light cream. Bring to the boil and turn off the heat. Correct the seasoning if necessary. In the last quarter of an hour, arrange the apples around the chicken.

When ready, cut up the chicken, coat with the reheated cream of cider and serve with the cinnamon apples.

138

Chicken with Cep Mushrooms

PREPARATION: 20 MINUTES
COOKING TIME: 45 MINUTES

SERVES: 4

INGREDIENTS:
2 young chickens,
  between 1¼ to 1¾ lb.
  each
8 nice, fresh cep
  mushrooms
juice of 1 lemon
1 tablespoon freshly
  chopped parsley
olive oil
salt, freshly ground
  pepper

Clean the mushrooms and cut into pieces.

Cut the young chickens into eight.

Heat the olive oil in a casserole. Add the chicken pieces and lightly brown all over, making sure the skin is properly cooked. This should take bout 12 minutes or so.

Add the mushrooms to the casserole and sprinkle with olive oil. Reduce the heat as low as possible, cover the casserole and cook for 30 minutes.

Half-way through the cooking, add the salt, pepper, and lemon juice.

Serve hot and decorate with the chopped parsley.

Chicken with Garlic

PREPARATION: 20 MINUTES
COOKING TIME: 1 HOUR 20 MINUTES

SERVES: 4

INGREDIENTS:

1 fresh young chicken weighing about 3 lb., with liver (or free-range chicken, if available)

4 heads of garlic (about 20 cloves)

1 large celery stalk

goose fat

salt, freshly ground pepper, cayenne

Recommended side dishes: Braised fennel
Diced celeriac browned
in goose fat

Brown the liver gently in a pan with goose fat.

Crush 5 cloves garlic and cut the celery stalk into small pieces.

Mix together in a blender the liver, crushed cloves of garlic, celery pieces, and 1 tablespoon of goose fat to make a purée. Season with salt and pepper.

Stuff the chicken with the mixture.

Place the chicken in an ovenware dish. Coat with the goose fat. Season with salt, pepper, and cayenne. Put in the oven (400°F) and cook for about 1 hour 15 minutes.

After 20 minutes in the oven, baste the chicken with a glassful of hot salted water. Put the rest of the garlic which had not been peeled, around the chicken and leave to cook until the end.

Chicken with Garlic Stuffing

PREPARATION: 30 MINUTES
COOKING TIME: 2 HOURS

SERVES: 5

INGREDIENTS:
1 fresh young chicken
weighing about 3¼ lb.
with liver and
gizzards (or free-range
chicken if available)
3 garlic heads
1 egg + yolk
salt, freshly ground
pepper, cayenne
goose fat
Herbs de Provence

Recommended side dishes: Braised chicory
Provençale tomatoes

Prepare the garlic cloves and cook in a steamer for 30 minutes.

Cut the liver and gizzards into very small pieces. Add a little goose fat to the pan and brown them over a medium heat.

Transfer to the blender. Add the garlic and the eggs. Season with salt, pepper, and cayenne.

Stuff the chicken with the coarse mixture and seal the rear end of the carcass with a ball of aluminum foil, or by sewing the opening together.

Brush the chicken with a tablespoon of goose fat. Season with salt and pepper, and dust with Herbs de Provence.

Place in the oven to cook (450°F) for 1 hour 15 minutes.

Half way through the cooking, pour a glassful of hot salted water into the roasting pan and baste the chicken with the cooking juices.

Cut up the chicken and slice the stuffing.

De-glaze the pan with hot water and serve the gravy separately.

141

Duck Breast Casserole

PREPARATION: 25 MINUTES
COOKING TIME: 1 HOUR 10 MINUTES

SERVES: 5

INGREDIENTS:
5 duck breasts
3 large onions - sliced thinly
4 cloves garlic
7 oz. can of mushrooms
5 oz. pickling onions or shallots - peeled
9 fl.oz. dry red wine
1 bouquet garni
salt, freshly ground pepper, cayenne
nutmeg

This dish can be prepared in advance. When the sauce had reached room temperature, the meat may be added and then reheated over a gentle heat.

With a very sharp knife, remove as much fat from the breasts as possible (do not leave more than about $\frac{1}{16}$ in.

In a casserole, melt the fat of two breasts over a low heat. Throw away the part that does not melt and only keep the equivalent of 3 tablespoons of fat.

In this fat, sear the duck breasts for 2 or 3 minutes - they must be crisp outside and pink inside. Season with salt and pepper. Take out the meat and reserve.

Brown the sliced onions in the casserole. Then add the garlic.

Pour in the red wine and add the bouquet garni. Season with salt, pepper, cayenne, and freshly grated nutmeg.

Cook uncovered to reduce.

Put 3½ oz. of mushrooms in the blender and chop finely. Add to the casserole together with the remainder of the mushrooms and the small onions.

Boil vigorously for 20 to 30 minutes to reduce the liquid.

When the sauce thickens, remove the bouquet garni and adjust the seasoning.

10 to 15 minutes before serving, return the duck breasts to the casserole. Cover and leave to simmer.

Duck Breasts in Bags

PREPARATION: 15 MINUTES
COOKING TIME: 15 MINUTES

SERVES: 4

INGREDIENTS:
4 duck breasts
7 fl.oz. tea cream
2 tablespoons strong
 mustard
salt, freshly ground
 pepper, cayenne
Herbs de Provence

Recommended side dishes: *Celeriac purée*
Parsley mushrooms
Provençale tomatoes

Place each breast fatty side downwards in the middle of a rectangle of aluminum foil. Season with salt, pepper, cayenne, and some Herbs de Provence. Draw the long edges of the foil together and close the bag by folding over a couple of times. Pinch the ends together and pull upwards to form a gondola.

Cook over the barbecue or grill, in an open fire or in a preheated oven (500°F). Cook for 5 to 10 minutes, depending on the method of cooking and the heat applied. If in doubt, partially open one of the bags after 6 minutes to check doneness.

When ready, carve the breasts into thin slices and keep warm, retaining 2 tablespoons of the cooking liquid to make the sauce.

Mix the liquid with the mustard and tea cream, pour over the duck slices and serve immediately.

143

Duck Breasts with Olives

PREPARATION: 15 MINUTES
COOKING TIME: 20 MINUTES

SERVES: 4

INGREDIENTS:
1 lb. green olives -
  stones removed
4 duck breasts
salt, freshly ground
  pepper, cayenne
olive oil

Recommended side dishes: *Parsley mushrooms*
Eggplant gratin
Zucchinis gratin

Purée 7 oz. olives in the blender with 1 tablespoon of olive oil.

Remove three-quarters of the fat covering the breasts. Use a third of the fat. Cut into cubes and melt slowly over a low heat. Discard the residue.

Add the olive purée. Season with salt and pepper, then add the rest of the olives and cook for 5 minutes.

For pink centers, fry the breasts in a non-stick pan for 6 minutes each side, starting with the fatty side. Vary the cooking time according to taste. Turn off the heat.

Cut the breasts into slices ½ in. thick, coat with the olive purée and serve on warm plates.

144

Duck Breasts with Orange

PREPARATION: 20 MINUTES
COOKING TIME: 15 MINUTES

SERVES: 4

INGREDIENTS:
4 duck breasts
3 oranges
juice of 2 oranges
zest of 1 orange
salt, freshly ground
  pepper

Using a very sharp knife, remove the fat from the duck breasts, leaving a thin film on the meat which is barely visible.

Dice the fat from one duck very finely. Discard the remainder.

In a casserole, melt the diced fat over a low heat.

Remove any residue with a slotted spoon.

Peel the oranges and cut into slices. Fry gently for 3 minutes in the duck fat.

In an ovenware dish, arrange the breasts with the fatty side facing up. Season with salt.

Spread the orange slices and zest around the duck, adding the juice of another 2 oranges.

Place under a pre-heated broiler (4 in.) for 6 minutes.

Transfer to a board and carve the slices about ¼ in. thick. Then, unless the breasts are preferred very pink, replace in the cooking dish and put in the oven (210°F) for a further 2 or 3 minutes.

Serve immediately.

145

Duck with Olives

PREPARATION: 20 MINUTES
COOKING TIME: 2 HOURS 10 MINUTES

SERVES: 4

INGREDIENTS:
1 large duck with the liver
11 oz. green olives - stones removed
11 oz. black olives - stones removed
2 eggs
2 slices wholemeal bread
4 fl.oz. light cream
1 onion - peeled
salt, freshly ground pepper, cayenne
olive oil

Cut up the liver and brown quickly in some olive oil.

Soak the bread in the light cream and allow to swell.

Use the blender to make a paste of the liver, a third of the green and black olives, the eggs, and the bread soaked in cream. Season with salt, Herbs de Provence, pepper, and cayenne.

Stuff the duck with this mixture and seal the body cavity with an onion.

Put the duck in a roasting tin. Sprinkle salt, pepper, and cayenne over the top and place in the oven (320°F).

After an hour, slowly pour a glass of salted water over the duck and then add the rest of the olives to the contents of the pan and stir together.

Return the duck to the oven and continue cooking at a reduced temperature (260°F) for another hour.

Remove the olives with a slotted spoon and reserve in a warm place. Skim-off some of the fat in the pan and de-glaze the remainder with a glassful of boiling water.

Carve the duck in the roasting pan, to conserve the juices. Arrange the pieces on a warm dish.

Finish de-glazing the roasting pan and reheat the sauce before pouring into a warm sauceboat.

146

Fillets of Turkey with Port

PREPARATION: 20 MINUTES
COOKING TIME: 30 MINUTES

SERVES: 4

INGREDIENTS:
4 turkey fillets
4 leek whites
2 shallots - chopped
7 fl.oz. chicken stock
7 fl.oz. light cream
2 tablespoons port
salt, pepper, cayenne
olive oil

Cut the leek whites into thin rings and fry them gently with the shallots in some olive oil in a casserole.

Add the chicken stock, light cream, port, salt, pepper, and cayenne. Cover and cook on a low heat for 10 minutes.

Put the turkey fillets into the casserole and cook over a medium heat for 10 minutes. Remove, arrange on a serving dish and reserve in a warm place.

Strain the leek whites in a colander and reserve the sauce. Purée the leeks and arrange around the meat on the serving dish.

Reduce the sauce till creamy. Pour over the meat and serve.

Flambé of Guinea Fowl with Chicory

PREPARATION: 25 MINUTES
COOKING TIME: 55 MINUTES

SERVES: 4

INGREDIENTS:
1 guinea fowl weighing
    2½ lb.
8 chicories
goose fat
½ glass brandy
4 fl.oz. light cream
salt, freshly ground
    pepper, cayenne

Coat the guinea fowl with goose fat. Season with salt, pepper, and cayenne.

Put in an ovenware dish and roast in the oven (450°F) for 55 minutes.

During this time, boil the chicory for 30 minutes in a pan of salted water. Drain well.

A quarter of an hour before the guinea fowl is cooked, add the chicory to the dish in the oven.

When the guinea fowl is done, remove from the oven. Take out the chicory and put on a serving dish.

Cut the guinea fowl into pieces in the oven dish and flambé with the brandy. Arrange the pieces of fowl on the serving dish with the chicory.

De-glaze the oven dish with the double cream and pour the sauce into a warm boat.

Cornish Hen in a Bag

PREPARATION: 20 MINUTES
COOKING TIME: 30 MINUTES

SERVES: 4

INGREDIENTS:
4 cornish hen - cleaned
  and plucked
4 tablespoons goose fat
aluminum foil
1 box of watercress
salt, freshly ground
  pepper

Recommended side dishes: Broccoli
French beans

Halve the cornish hen down their length.

Coat with goose fat. Season with salt and pepper.

Place each half on a foil sheet, which should be folded over at the edges to form a bag.

Place the aluminum bags in a pre-heated oven (400°F) and cook for 30 minutes.

Serve the cornish hen on plates decorated with watercress.

149

Cornish Hen with Cabbage

PREPARATION: 30 MINUTES
COOKING TIME: 2 HOURS

SERVES: 4

INGREDIENTS:
2 cornish hen
2 slices fat bacon
1 firm savoy cabbage
9 oz. diced marbled
   bacon
1 onion
1 bouquet garni
7 fl.oz. chicken stock
2 tablespoons goose fat
salt, pepper

Tie the fat slices over the cornish hen breasts.

In a large pan, bring 3 lb. of salted water to the boil.

Remove the outer leaves of the cabbage and cut the heart into four quarters.

Blanche for 10 minutes in the boiling water. Drain.

In a large casserole melt the goose fat. Cook the quartered onion and diced marbled bacon for a few minutes, until golden. Remove with a slotted spoon and keep warm.

In the same casserole, cook the cornish hens over a medium heat for 15 minutes until brown all over. Season with salt and pepper.

Remove the cornish hens and replace with the cabbage. Season with salt and pepper and add the bouquet garni. Add a little bouillon and allow to simmer for about 15 minutes.

Remove the cabbage and throw away the bouquet garni.

Spread out half the cabbage on a large ovenware dish. Place the cornish hens on top with the diced marbled bacon. Cover with the remainder of the cabbage and pour the cooking juices over the top. Cover with a sheet of foil and cook in a very hot oven (500°F) for about 1 hour.

Chicken with Sauerkraut

PREPARATION: 30 MINUTES
COOKING TIME: 1 HOUR 45 MINUTES

SERVES: 4

INGREDIENTS:

2 small cockerel (fresh young roasting chicken) plucked and cleaned

2 broad slices of fat bacon

2½ lb. raw sauerkraut

10½ oz. diced marbled bacon

2 small onions

1 bouquet garni

juniper berries

peppercorns

goose fat

dry white wine

½ glass brandy

salt and freshly ground pepper

Wash the sauerkraut. Press and drain well.

In a casserole, brown the diced marbled bacon with the quartered onions.

Add the bouquet garni, a dozen juniper berries, and some peppercorns.

Then add the sauerkraut. Pour in enough wine to cover the sauerkraut. Bring to the boil, then cover and put the casserole in the oven (260°F) for about an hour.

Tie the bacon fat onto the breast of each cockerel. Season all over with salt and pepper.

In a second casserole, heat 2 tablespoons of goose fat. Brown the cockerel all over and when golden brown, cover and continue cooking on a gentle heat for 20 minutes.

Remove the sauerkraut from the oven to see whether it is cooked - it should be translucent. Drain and discard the onion and bouquet garni. Arrange on the serving dish and reserve in a warm place.

Cut the cockerel in half and flambé with the brandy.

Remove the string and place the pheasants on the bed of sauerkraut. De-glaze the casserole in which the cockerel were cooked with a little of the white wine and pour this over the dish or into the sauceboat. Serve immediately.

151

Chicken with Garden Peas

PREPARATION: 20 MINUTES
COOKING TIME: 55 MINUTES

SERVES: 4

INGREDIENTS:
4 cockerel (fresh young roasting chicken) plucked and cleaned
2 onions - sliced
5 fl.oz. dry white wine
5 fl.oz. chicken stock
1 lb. petite peas
4 oz. cured ham - in slices about ¼ in. thick
2 tablespoons goose fat
salt, freshly ground pepper, cayenne

Cut the ham into small cubes.

Season the inside of the carcasses with salt, pepper, and cayenne.

Melt the goose fat in a large casserole. Put in the onions and brown gently for 2 or 3 minutes. Add the cockerel and cook until golden all over.

Pour in the wine and add the ham. Cook over a low heat for 10 minutes.

Add the chicken stock and cover. Cook over a very gentle heat for 20 minutes.

Add the petite peas and simmer for another 15 minutes.

Serve in a deep dish together with all the cooking juices.

152

Chicken with Thyme Stuffing

PREPARATION: 20 MINUTES
COOKING TIME: 45 MINUTES

SERVES: 4

INGREDIENTS:
4 young cockerel (fresh
   young roasting
   chicken)
4 shallots - sliced
8 cloves garlic - sliced
1 large bunch fresh
   thyme
1 bunch parsley
½ glass brandy
goose fat
salt, freshly ground
   pepper

Recommended side dish: Sweet pepper purée

Have the cockerel plucked and cleaned, and the lower leg and neck removed. Ask for the livers, gizzards, and hearts. If not available, buy 7 oz. of chicken liver instead.

Cut the livers, gizzards, and hearts into small pieces and cook in a little goose fat seasoned with salt and pepper.

In the same pan, brown the shallots and garlic - adding a little goose fat if necessary.

Blend the livers, gizzards, hearts, garlic, shallots with their cooking juices, as well as the thyme and the parsley, to make the stuffing.

Divide the mixture equally between the four pigeons and stuff.

Brush the four birds with goose fat. Season with salt and pepper. Then cook in a preheated oven (375°F) for 30 to 35 minutes.

Half-way through the cooking, baste with a small glassful of hot salted water.

When cooked, remove the cockerel from the oven and cut in two on a board. Put them back in the cooking pan and flambé with brandy.

Serve at once.

153

Roast Breast of Duck

PREPARATION: 20 MINUTES
COOKING TIME: 25 MINUTES

SERVES: 4

INGREDIENTS:
3 duck's breasts
2 cloves garlic - peeled
salt, freshly ground
    pepper
Herbs de Provence

Recommended side dishes: Small broad beans
Parsley mushrooms
Cep mushrooms

Remove all the fat from one of the three breasts, by pulling the fat with one hand and cutting the securing membrane with the tip of a sharp knife in the other. Season all three breasts with salt, pepper, and herbs.

Then make up the roast by sandwiching the stripped breast between the other two, leaving their fatty parts facing outwards. Tie together with string to secure.

Halve the garlic cloves and insert into the meat by making a deep and narrow slit with the point of a sharp knife.

Put the duck breasts in a pan and place in the oven (450°F). Cook for 25 minutes. After 15, remove as much fat as possible from the bottom of the pan. Then pour half a glass of hot salted water over the roast.

When cooked, take the duck out of the oven and slice like rolled beef. Like beef, the center should be hot and very pink. Serve with the cooking juices and carving juices mixed together.

Variation:

The cooking tin can also be de-glazed with whipping cream, seasoned with salt, pepper, and a pinch of cayenne.

154

Sauté of Foie Gras and Parsley Mushrooms

PREPARATION: 20 MINUTES
COOKING TIME: 20 MINUTES

SERVES: 4

INGREDIENTS:
1 lb. 2 oz. foie gras (goose liver)
1¼ lb. button mushrooms
5 cloves garlic - crushed
3 tablespoons chopped parsley
4 tablespoons sherry vinegar
salt, freshly ground pepper

Ideally this dish should be made with fresh foie gras.

Clean and slice the mushrooms.

In a large frying pan, heat the oil and sauté the mushrooms. Season with salt and pepper.

When the mushrooms have reduced, discard the cooking juices. Replace with fresh olive oil.

On one side of the frying pan, fry the garlic and parsley over a low heat. Stir into the mushrooms. Reserve and keep warm.

Cut the foie gras down its length into slices 1 in. thick and cook over a low heat in a non-stick pan for about 1 minute on each side. Season with salt and pepper. Remove and reserve on very hot plates.

Discard about half of the fat released by the foie gras. De-glaze the frying pan with the sherry vinegar. Add the mushrooms. Mix well and serve with the foie gras.

155

Stuffed Goose with Chestnuts

PREPARATION: 30 MINUTES
COOKING TIME: 3 HOURS 45 MINUTES

SERVES: 10

INGREDIENTS:
1 goose weighing 6½ lb.
  - with liver if possible
4½ lb. fresh chestnuts
2 pints chicken stock
3 tablespoons of tea
  cream
2 bay leaves
14 fl.oz. whipping cream
salt, freshly ground
  pepper, chili pepper
Herbs de Provence

Add the bay leaves to the chicken stock and bring to the boil. Add the peeled chestnuts and simmer for 35 minutes. Drain and reserve.

Brown the goose liver in a pan with some goose fat. Salt, pepper, and add some Herbs de Provence. (If you cannot come by the goose liver, substitute with 18 oz. chicken livers and cook the same way).

Blend together the liver, slightly less than half the chestnuts, and the tea cream into a coarse paste. Adjust the seasoning, making sure there is enough ground pepper and chili pepper.

Fill the goose with this stuffing and secure by sewing up the rear opening.

Put the goose in a large tin and place in the oven. Cook in a warm oven (320°F) for at least 3 hours.

While the goose is cooking, remove the dripping which should be stored for future use.

In the last half hour, add the remainder of the chestnuts.

When cooking is completed, remove most of the fat from the pan and de-glaze with the whipping cream. Pour the sauce into a boat to accompany the goose.

Turkey Escalopes with Cream

PREPARATION: 10 MINUTES
COOKING TIME: 20 MINUTES

SERVES: 4

INGREDIENTS:
4 good slices of turkey
    breast
4 fl.oz. dry white wine
1 container (4 oz.)
    yogurt
1 tablespoon mustard
goose fat
1 tablespoon freshly
    chopped parsley

Recommended side dishes: Spinach
French beans

Fry the turkey slices in the goose fat over a medium heat until golden brown.

Season with salt and pepper. Reserve and keep warm on the serving dish.

De-glaze the pan with the white wine. Boil down slightly, then add the yogurt mixed with the mustard. Stir over a gentle heat.

Coat the escalopes with the sauce and sprinkle with parsley.

157

Turkey Pot-au-Feu

PREPARATION: 15 MINUTES
COOKING TIME: 1 HOUR 20 MINUTES

SERVES: 6

INGREDIENTS:
6 turkey thighs
3 large onions - sliced
1 small celeriac
9 oz. French beans
14 fl.oz. chicken stock
3 tablespoons goose fat
bouquet garni
salt, freshly ground
   pepper

Put the goose fat in a casserole and brown the sliced onions for a few minutes over a gentle heat.

Meanwhile, cut the celeriac into cubes and cut the french beans into short lengths. Put them in the casserole and mix with the onions. Continue cooking for several minutes.

Arrange the pieces of turkey next to each other on top of the vegetables. Season with salt, pepper, and add the bouquet garni. Pour the chicken stock over the top. Raise the heat and bring to the boil. Cover and simmer for 1 hour.

Serve when cooked. Alternatively, allow to get cold so that the fat can be removed easily. Reheat when required.

Turkey with Apples

PREPARATION: 30 MINUTES
COOKING TIME: 2 HOURS 40 MINUTES

SERVES: 8

INGREDIENTS:
1 turkey weighing 8 lb.
1¼ lb. sliced onions
3¼ lb. apples (cox)
4 cloves garlic - chopped
6 leaves fresh sage
goose fat
olive oil
1 lemon
salt, freshly ground
   pepper, cayenne
1 glass cider
7 fl. oz. light cream

In a frying pan brown the onions in olive oil. Add the garlic towards the end.

Peel and quarter the apples. Squeeze lemon over them to prevent them from turning brown. Cook one third of the apples in the goose fat over a low heat.

Chop the sage and add the onions, garlic, and apples to make a stuffing. Season with salt, pepper, and cayenne.

Stuff the turkey and sew up the opening. Coat the turkey with the goose fat. Season with salt, pepper, and sprinkle lightly with cayenne.

Put in a roasting pan, adding a good glass of water and place in a fairly hot oven (375°F). Cook for 2 hours and 15 minutes, basting every 30 minutes.

During the last half-hour, pour off the cooking juices and add the rest of the peeled and quartered apples. Pour a quarter of the cooking juices carefully over the apples, reserving the rest to make the sauce.

When the turkey is done, de-glaze the roasting pan with the cider, stirring in the reserved juices together with the cream.

159

Fish

161

Cod Provençale

PREPARATION: 10 MINUTES
COOKING TIME: 50 MINUTES

SERVES: 4

INGREDIENTS:
1½ lb. salted cod
4 shallots - sliced
9 fl. oz. dry white wine
9 fl. oz. fish stock
2 tablespoons tomato
  paste
1 sprig thyme
1 tablespoon freshly
  chopped parsley
1 tablespoon freshly
  chopped basil
5 oz. green olives -
  stoned
2 bay leaves
salt, freshly ground
  pepper

Recommended side dishes: Leeks
                    French beans

Immerse the fish in water for 24 hours to remove salt, changing the water every 6 hours.

In a deep frying pan or wok, brown the shallots and garlic in live oil. Stir in the tomato paste. Add the wine, fish stock, thyme, parsley, basil, and bay leaves. Bring to the boil and then cook over a gentle heat for 20 minutes.

Drain the fish and cut into 4 pieces. Cook over a low heat in a non-stick pan with olive oil.

When the sauce had reduced to a half, adjust the seasoning.

Reheat the cod by cooking in the sauce for a few minutes.

Serve very hot.

Fillets of Sole with Cream of Soy Sauce

PREPARATION: 20 MINUTES
COOKING TIME: 20 MINUTES

SERVES: 4

INGREDIENTS:
4 large fillets of sole
juice of 1 lemon
5 oz. button mushrooms, washed and sliced
7 fl. oz. soy cream
4 oz. peeled prawns
1 egg yolk
olive oil
salt, freshly ground pepper
1 tablespoon fresh parsley

Recommended side dishes: Spinach
French beans

Wash the fillets under the faucet and pat dry with absorbent kitchen paper.

Heat 2 tablespoons of olive oil in a non-stick frying pan, and gently fry the fish. Pour lemon juice over the top. Season with salt and pepper. Continue cooking over a low heat for 2 minutes. Set aside and keep warm.

Fry the mushrooms over a gentle heat in 2 tablespoons of olive oil.

Discard the cooking juices and the water from the mushrooms. Add the cream of soy, mixed beforehand in a bowl with the egg yolk. Season with salt and pepper. Add the prawns.

Continue cooking over a low heat for a few minutes, stirring continuously.

Arrange the fish on warmed plates and coat with the sauce.

163

Fillets of Sole with Salmon

PREPARATION: 15 MINUTES
COOKING TIME: 20 MINUTES

SERVES: 4

INGREDIENTS:
4 good sized sole fillets
10 oz. fillet of salmon
5 shallots - sliced
3 tablespoons sour cream
5 fl. oz. dry white wine
juice of ½ lemon
1 tablespoon freshly
  chopped parsley

Recommended side dishes: *Broccoli*
Spinach
French beans

Ask the grocer to fillet the sole and then to slice the salmon fillets thinly as for smoked salmon.

Take a fillet of sole and cover with a fillet of salmon and roll the two together. Secure by spiking with a wooden toothpick.

In a pan, brown the shallots a few minutes in olive oil. Then add the white wine. Season with salt and pepper and cook for 1 minute.

Put the fish rolls in an ovenware dish. Season with salt and pepper. Pour the wine mixture over the top.

Place in a fairly hot oven (375°F) for 12 to 15 minutes.

Take out of the oven and arrange the fish on a serving dish. Reserve in warm place.

Quickly add the sour cream and the lemon juice to the cooking juices in the ovenware dish and blend with a fork.

Coat the fish rolls with the sauce and decorate with parsley before serving.

164

Fish Soup with Shellfish

PREPARATION: 30 MINUTES
COOKING TIME: 40 MINUTES

SERVES: 5-6

INGREDIENTS:

4½ lb. assorted fish (monkfish, conger eel, bream, hake, mullet, cod, etc.)

12 prawns, tiger prawns or giant scampi - uncooked

2 pints mussels

4 white leeks

1 stalk of celery with leaves removed

1 onion

3 shallots

3 cloves garlic

1 bouquet garni

3 tablespoons of sour cream

olive oil

sea salt, peppercorns, cayenne

Have the fish cleaned, de-scaled and trimmed by the grocer. Cut into sections (very large slices).

Clean the mussels in several changes of water. Remove the beards and throw away any broken shells. Then, leaving them in a very large pan of clean water, throw away those that rise to the surface or do not close.

Peel, wash, and chop finely the celery, leeks, onion, shallots, and garlic.

In a large casserole, heat 3 tablespoons of olive oil and sweat the vegetables for 5 minutes.

Add 3 pints water, the bouquet garni, salt, peppercorns, and 3 good pinches of cayenne. Simmer the soup for 15 to 20 minutes with the lid removed.

Add the fish to the soup: first, the fish with solid flesh (monkfish, conger eel) and then about 5 minutes later, the fish with fine grained flesh (hake, cod, bream, mullet, etc.).

Add the mussels and the prawns 2 minutes later and cook for a further 3 to 5 minutes.

With a slotted spoon, recover the fish and shellfish and keep warm in a soup tureen.

Remove the bouquet garni from the soup. Adjust the seasoning and add the sour cream. Cook for 1 or 2 minutes and pour over the fish. Serve immediately.

165

Grilled Salmon Fillets with Tamari

PREPARATION: 10 MINUTES
COOKING TIME: 10 MINUTES

SERVES: 4

INGREDIENTS:
1¾ lb. salmon fillets
juice of 1 lemon
olive oil
tamari (thick soy sauce)
fine sea salt
pepper, Herbs de Provence

Recommended side dish: *Leeks with olive oil dressing*

Cut the fillets into 4 equal pieces. Brush with olive oil. Season with salt and pepper.

Pre-heat the broiler.

Place the fillet pieces in an ovenware dish with the skin facing uppermost. Sprinkle lightly with Herbs de Provence.

Broil for 10 minutes.

Meanwhile, prepare the sauce: mix together the lemon juice, olive oil, tamari, a pinch of sea salt, and a pinch of pepper.

Arrange the salmon on the plates, with the skin side down. Sprinkle with parsley. Stir the sauce well, pour over the top and serve.

Grilled Sea Bass with Fennel Flamed with Pastis

PREPARATION: 20 MINUTES
COOKING TIME: 40 MINUTES

SERVES: 4-5

INGREDIENTS:
1 sea bass weighing 3½ to 4½ lb.
fennel stalks
olive oil
3 cloves garlic - crushed
½ glass pastis (Pernod)
salt, freshly ground pepper, cayenne
3 lemons

*Recommended side dishes: Braised fennel
Leeks sautéed in olive oil*

Have the fish cleaned and de-scaled by your grocer.

Make a marinade with the olive oil, crushed garlic, salt, pepper, and cayenne. Brush liberally in the body cavity and fill completely with fennel stalks.

Place some fennel stalks on the bottom of a roasting tin and lay the fish on top. Brush the sea bass liberally with the marinade.

Put the fish under the broiler for 15 to 20 minutes. Allow to char. Turn, brush with the marinade again and cook for a further 15 or 20 minutes.

Transfer the fish to a serving dish and remove the fennel stalks.

Flambé with the pastis.

If desired, the fish may be served with a dressing of olive oil, lemon juice, salt and pepper.

Note:

This is an ideal recipe for a barbecue. Be careful however, not to overcook the fish and be prepared to use aluminum foil to prevent the flesh getting dry and fibrous.

Hake Country Style

PREPARATION: 20 MINUTES
COOKING TIME: 1 HOUR 10 MINUTES

SERVES: 4-5

INGREDIENTS:
1 hake weighing about
3¼ lb.
2¼ lb. fresh petite peas
(or frozen)
2 small celeriac
10 silver skin onions
1 lb. asparagus tips
4 cloves garlic - sliced
olive oil
salt, freshly ground
pepper, cayenne

Ask the grocer to clean the hake and cut it into slices 1 in. thick.

Prepare the vegetables. Ideally, steam the asparagus and the petite peas in a two-tiered steamer. Alternatively, cook in boiling water.

Cook the celeriac and silver skin onions for 30 to 40 minutes in a small amount of water with olive oil and salt.

In a small pan, brown the sliced garlic in 2 tablespoons of olive oil.

Pour garlic and oil into an ovenware dish. Add the slices of hake and lay flat. Season with salt, pepper, and cayenne. Place about 4 in. below the broiler and cook for 5 to 10 minutes.

Arrange the peas, asparagus, celeriac, and onions in a terra cotta dish, and then add the slices of hake. Drizzle fresh olive oil on the top and serve.

Lemon Sole Cretan Style

PREPARATION: 10 MINUTES
COOKING TIME: 10 MINUTES

SERVES: 4

INGREDIENTS:
6 lemon sole fillets
3 onions - sliced
3 lemons
4 bay leaves
2 sprigs thyme
1 glass olive oil
salt, freshly ground
    pepper

Recommended side dish: Brussels sprouts

Prepare a marinade with the olive oil, sliced onions, lemon juice, thyme, bay leaf, salt, and pepper.

Marinate the fish fillets for 20 minutes.

Then pour the marinade in a frying pan over a medium heat. When the marinade is hot, add the fillets and poach for 5 minutes each side.

Serve with a dressing of olive oil and lemon juice according to taste.

Monkfish American Style

PREPARATION: 20 MINUTES
COOKING TIME: 40 MINUTES

SERVES: 4

INGREDIENTS:
3½ lb. boned monkfish
18 fl. oz. dry white wine
2 tablespoons tomato paste
4 shallots - sliced
3½ oz. crushed tomatoes (canned)
olive oil
salt, freshly ground pepper
2 fl. oz. brandy

Cut the monkfish into short lengths of 2 in. and in a non-stick pan, brown in olive oil over a low heat.

Season with salt, pepper and flambé with the brandy.

De-glaze the pan with a tablespoon of dry white wine. Reserve and keep warm.

In a deep frying pan or wok, soften the sliced shallots and garlic with 2 tablespoons of olive oil. Add the tomato paste and simmer for a few minutes, stirring frequently.

Add the rest of the white wine. Season with salt and pepper.

Cover and bring to the boil. Remove the lid and simmer for 10 minutes.

Add the drained tomato pieces and finally the fish. Bring back to the boil and serve immediately.

170

Normandy Sole

PREPARATION: 15 MINUTES
COOKING TIME: 20 MINUTES

SERVES: 4

INGREDIENTS:
6 large fillets of sole
1 pint milk
4 oz. peeled prawns
7 oz. canned button
  mushrooms
1 egg yolk
7 fl. oz. sour cream
1 lemon
salt, pepper

Recommended side dishes: Spinach
French beans

Poach the fillets in milk and simmer very gently for 10 minutes. Drain, reserve, and keep warm.

In a pan, mix the prawns, drained button mushrooms, sour cream, and lemon juice. Warm through over a gentle heat for 5 minutes.

Away from the heat, add the egg yolks, stirring vigorously. Season very sparingly with pepper and salt, then pour over the fillets of sole and serve immediately.

171

Octopus with Onions

PREPARATION: 15 MINUTES
COOKING TIME: 2 HOURS 10 MINUTES

SERVE: 5

INGREDIENTS:
2¼ lb. prepared octopus
1 lb. silver skin onions - skinned
5 big tomatoes
3 tablespoons sherry vinegar
4 cloves garlic - crushed
2 bay leaves
1 glass dry white wine
3 pinches cinnamon

Place the octopus in a casserole of water and cook for 30 minutes.

Drain and cut into small pieces.

Pour boiling water on the tomatoes. Then peel, halve, and remove the seeds. Cut the flesh into large cubes.

Warm 3 tablespoons of olive oil in a casserole and brown the chopped octopus for 10 minutes. Add the garlic and cook a further 1 or 2 minutes, stirring well.

Then put in the vinegar, tomatoes, bay leaves, white wine, salt, pepper, and cinnamon. Cook over a gentle heat for 30 minutes. Add the onions, cover and cook for a good hour.

Red Mullet with Aniseed

PREPARATION: 15 MINUTES
COOKING TIME: 20 MINUTES

SERVES: 4

INGREDIENTS:
4 red mullet, cleaned, de-scaled and pared
14 oz. fennel
1 teaspoon aniseed grains
olive oil
salt, freshly ground pepper

Clean the fennel and cut into strips. Blanch in boiling salted water for 6 minutes. Drain well.

In an oven-proof dish, make a bed of fennel using half the strips. Place the fish on top. Cover with the remainder of the fennel. Sprinkle the aniseed grains over the dish and drizzle with olive oil. Season with salt and pepper.

Place in a very hot oven (500°F) for about 12 minutes.

Serve in the oven-proof dish.

Red Mullet with a Fresh Mint Sauce

PREPARATION: 15 MINUTES
COOKING TIME: 15 MINUTES

SERVES: 4

INGREDIENTS:
8 red mullet cleaned and de-scaled
4 oz. freshly chopped mint
6 cloves garlic
2 fl. oz. old wine vinegar
2 fl. oz. balsamic vinegar
3 tablespoons olive oil
salt, freshly ground pepper

Recommended side dishes: Braised chicory
Broccoli purée

Pre-heat the oven to a very cool 150°F.

Using a non-stick pan, add 2 tablespoons olive oil and cook the red mullet 4 minutes each side. Season with salt and pepper during the cooking.

Reserve and keep warm in the oven.

Slice the garlic very finely.

Pour the two vinegars and 1 tablespoon of olive oil into a pan. Add the garlic and chopped mint. Season lightly with salt and pepper.

Bring to the boil and stir for 4 to 5 minutes.

Remove the red mullet from the oven, pour the sauce over the fish and serve.

Red Mullet with a Wine and Cream Sauce

PREPARATION: 20 MINUTES
COOKING TIME: 20 MINUTES

SERVES: 4

INGREDIENTS:
8 nice red mullet fillets
juice of 1 lemon
3 shallots - sliced
1 glass dry white wine
7 fl. oz. sour cream
sea salt, freshly ground
    pepper
olive oil
1 tablespoon freshly
    chopped parsley

Recommended side dishes: Leeks sautéed in olive oil
French bean purée

Fry the shallots in olive oil over a low heat. When they are well softened without caramelizing, add the white wine. Raise the temperature to reduce the liquid by half. Season with salt and pepper. Reserve.

Wash the fillets under the faucet. Pat them dry with absorbent kitchen paper and then lay flat in a large dish. Squeeze the lemon over the fish.

Preheat 2 tablespoons of olive oil in a non-stick frying pan over a very low heat.

Cook the fillets on both sides. Season with salt and pepper.

Meanwhile, add the sour cream to the reserved onion mixture. Cook over a gentle heat and allow to thicken, stirring regularly.

Arrange the fillets on individual plates and coat with the sauce. Sprinkle with parsley and serve.

175

Salmon in a Salt Crust

PREPARATION: 10 MINUTES
COOKING TIME: 40 MINUTES

SERVES: 4

INGREDIENTS:
1 really fresh salmon
    weighing 2½ lb.
4½ lb. coarse sea salt
juice of 3 lemons
4 fl. oz. olive oil
salt, freshly ground
    pepper

Recommended side dishes: Chicory with soy cream
Leeks
Broccoli

Have the salmon cleaned and de-scaled by the grocer, but leave the head on.

On an oven tray or oven-proof dish large enough to accommodate the fish, lay a thin bed of salt. Place the fish on top and cover entirely with salt to a depth of at least ½ in.

Pre-heat the oven (500°F) and cook for 40 minutes.

When ready, break the crust gently and lift off together with the skin, using a large broad knife.

Make a dressing by mixing the olive oil, lemon, salt, and pepper. Pour the dressing over the fish and serve.

Sea Bass Fillets with Shallot Sauce

PREPARATION: 20 MINUTES
COOKING TIME: 5 MINUTES

SERVES: 4

INGREDIENTS:
2¼ lb. sea bass fillets
4 shallots
2 tablespoons olive oil
7 fl. oz. light cream

For the fish stock:
 use the head and
 bones
1 onion
1 stalk of celery
2 sprigs parsley
1 bouquet garni
½ glass dry white wine
½ glass red wine vinegar
salt, pepper

Recommended side dishes: *Broccoli*
 Spinach
 Cauliflower

Ask the grocer to prepare the fillets and reserve the head and bones for making the fish stock.

To prepare the fish stock, chop up the onion, celery and parsley.

Add the chopped vegetables to 2 ½ pints of water together with the bouquet garni, and boil for 30 minutes. Add the white wine and the vinegar. Allow to cool and pass through a conical stainer.

Add the fish head and bones to the stock. Bring to the boil and continue to reduce over a low heat, until all that remains is a glassful. Season with salt and pepper.

Liquefy the shallots and mix with the olive oil.

In an ovenware dish that has been lightly oiled, place the fillets with the skin side downwards. Season with salt and pepper. Spread the shallot and oil mixture on the fillets.

Place in the oven 4 in. below the broiler, and cook for 6 to 7 minutes.

Mix the glass of fish stock with the cream and adjust seasoning. Cook gently for 1 minute. Coat the fillets with the sauce and serve.

177

Sea Bream Basque Style

PREPARATION: 20 MINUTES
COOKING TIME: 25 MINUTES

SERVES: 4

INGREDIENTS:
2 sea bream weighing between 1¼ and 1½ lb. each
5 cloves garlic - sliced thinly
½ glass sherry vinegar
2 lemons
olive oil
1 bunch parsley
salt, freshly ground pepper, cayenne

Recommended side dishes: Ratatouille
Provençale tomatoes

Ask the grocer to scale and clean the bream.

Stuff with parsley and 2 or 3 lemon slices. Season with salt, pepper, and cayenne.

Arrange in an ovenware dish, brush with olive oil and place in the oven (375°F). Cook for 20 minutes - turning after 10 minutes, to cook the other side.

Fillet the sea bream. Arrange on warm plates. Squeeze lemon juice over the top and reserve in a warm place.

Immediately put the sliced garlic in a pan with 3 tablespoons olive oil. Cook until barely golden. Season with salt, pepper, and cayenne. At the last moment, add the sherry vinegar. Pour the boiling sauce over the fish and serve at once.

Squid Provençale

PREPARATION: 15 MINUTES
COOKING TIME: 45 MINUTES

SERVES: 4-5

INGREDIENTS:
2½ lb. squid
14 oz. green mild chillies
6 ripe tomatoes
5 gloves garlic
olive oil
salt, freshly ground
   pepper, cayenne

Ask the grocer to prepare the squid, leaving just the body and the tentacles.

Drop the tomatoes in boiling water for 30 seconds before removing the skins. Halve and remove the seeds. Cut the flesh into large cubes and reduce over a very low heat in a casserole containing 2 tablespoons of olive oil. Season with salt and pepper, then reserve.

Fry the green chillies very gently in olive oil for at least 20 minutes. Season with salt and pepper. In the last 5 minutes, add the sliced garlic and cook until pale golden, making certain it does not burn.

Fry the tentacles and body of the squid over a gentle heat in some olive oil. Season with salt, pepper, and cayenne.

Turn out the chillies and garlic with their cooking juices into a serving dish. Add the squid and cover with the tomato sauce. Mix well and simmer in the oven for 15 minutes in a very cool oven set at 160°F. Serve on warm plates.

179

Swordfish on Skewers

PREPARATION: 20 MINUTES
COOKING TIME: 15 MINUTES

SERVES: 4

INGREDIENTS:
2¼ lb. of prepared
  swordfish
4 firm tomatoes
2 onions
4 green peppers
olive oil
oregano, salt, freshly
  ground pepper
Herbs de Provence

Recommended side dishes: Ratatouille
Green salad

Cut the fish into 1 in. cubes.

Quarter the tomatoes and onions.

Cut open the peppers, remove the stalks and seeds, and cut into 1 in. squares.

Load the skewers as follows: pepper, tomato, onion, swordfish, onion, tomato...

Arrange on an ovenware dish. Brush with olive oil and sprinkle with Herbs de Provence, salt, freshly ground pepper, and oregano.

Place about 4 in. under the broiler and cook for about 15 minutes. Turn occasionally and baste regularly with the cooking juices.

Trout with Almonds

PREPARATION: 10 MINUTES
COOKING TIME: 15 MINUTES

SERVES: 4

INGREDIENTS:
4 plump trout
3 oz. flaked almonds
2 lemons
1 tablespoon sherry
    vinegar
2 tablespoons freshly
    chopped parsley
olive oil
salt, freshly ground
    pepper
Herbs de Provence

*Recommended side dishes: Zucchinis with olive oil
dressing
Spinach with soy cream*

Have the trout cleaned by the grocer.

Dust the body cavity with Herbs de Provence. Season with salt and pepper.

In a non-stick frying pan, gently heat 4 tablespoons of olive oil.

Place the trout in the pan and cook for 6 minutes on each side. Reserve and keep warm on a serving dish in a very cool oven at 175-200°F.

In another pan, add 1 tablespoon of olive oil and fry the almonds until golden brown. Season with salt and pepper. Add the sherry vinegar.

Pour the vinegar and almond mixture over the trout.

Serve with lemons cut into halves.

181

Tuna Tartare

PREPARATION: 20 MINUTES
NO COOKING

SERVES: 4

INGREDIENTS:
2¼ lb. very fresh tuna
4 shallots - very finely
  chopped
2 lemons
3 tablespoons olive oil
1 bunch fresh coriander
3 tablespoons freshly
  chopped parsley
1 tablespoon chopped
  chives
salt, freshly ground
  pepper
1 teaspoon cayenne

Prepare the tuna by removing the skin and all the bones.

Cut the flesh into small ¼ in. cubes. Season with salt, pepper, and cayenne. Pour olive oil over the top and mix well.

Add the chopped shallots, parsley and chives. Refrigerate for 1 or 2 hours.

Serve with a green salad. Before eating, squeeze the juice of 2 lemons over the dish.

Tuna, Tomato, and Scrambled Egg

PREPARATION: 15 MINUTES
COOKING TIME: 45 MINUTES

SERVES: 4

INGREDIENTS:
1 lb. tuna in brine
1 lb. tomato sauce (coulis)
1 lb. tomatoes, blanched, skinned, de-seeded and diced
1 shallot, finely sliced
1 clove garlic - crushed
1 tablespoon olive oil
1 sachet Herbs de Provence
3 egg yolks + 1 egg
4 cloves garlic - crushed
3 tablespoons freshly chopped parsley
4 tablespoons olive oil
7 fl. oz. heavy cream

Recommended side dishes: *Green salad*
                              Chicory salad

Drain the tuna.

Purée the tuna, garlic, parsley, and 4 tablespoons olive oil in a food processor. Reserve.

Put the tomato sauce (see below for instructions on how to make the sauce) in a double-boiler with the eggs and cream. Cook, whisking the mixture all the time until it thickens.

Add the tuna purée and blend with a spatula.

Pour into an soufflé dish and place in a very cool oven (250°F) for 30 to 35 minutes.

Before serving, sprinkle with grated gruyere cheese and place under the broiler for a few minutes.

Serve immediately.

183

To make the sauce (coulis):

(add a further 15 to 20 minutes to the overall cooking time, if the sauce is made while preparing the dish) Sauté the shallots and garlic with the olive oil in a pan over a low heat for 4 minutes or until transparent. Add the tomatoes and sachet of herbs and simmer for 10 to 12 minutes. Remove the sachet and purée the mixture in the blender. Return to the heat, bring to the boil. Adjust seasoning and simmer for a further 5 minutes.

Tuna with Garlic Vinegar

PREPARATION: 15 MINUTES
COOKING TIME: 20 MINUTES

SERVES: 4

INGREDIENTS:
2 thick slices of fresh
   tuna - weighing about
   1¾ lb. in all
4 cloves garlic - finely
   sliced
olive oil
sherry vinegar
salt, freshly ground
   pepper

*Recommended side dishes: Eggplant gratin
                            Cauliflower*

Heat 2 or 3 tablespoons olive oil in a non-stick frying pan. Fry the tuna steaks for 4 or 5 minutes on each side. Season with salt and pepper. Reserve in a very cool oven - 150°F.

Throw away the cooking oil and de-glaze the pan with 3 tablespoons of sherry vinegar. Reserve.

In another pan, brown the garlic slices in tablespoons of olive oil over a low heat. Season with salt.

Pour the reserved vinegar de-glazing into the pan with the garlic. Raise the temperature slightly for between 30 to 60 seconds. Then pour over the tuna steaks.

184

Turbot with Fennel

PREPARATION: 25 MINUTES
COOKING TIME: 15 MINUTES

SERVES: 4

INGREDIENTS:
4 turbot fillets weighing together about 1¾ lb.
6 good-sized tomatoes
1 bulb fennel
juice of 4 lemons
10 fl. oz. fish stock
4 finely sliced shallots
1 clove garlic - crushed
2 oz. sour cream
olive oil
salt, pepper, thyme

Wash the fillets under the faucet. Pat dry with absorbent kitchen paper.

Wash the fennel. Cut into fine strips.

Drop the tomatoes in boiling water for 30 seconds, peel and remove the seeds. Cut the flesh into strips.

Brown the fennel, garlic, and shallots in a casserole with olive oil. Then cover and sweat a few minutes.

In a medium-sized casserole, heat the lemon juice and fish stock. Season with salt and pepper. Add the thyme. Poach the turbot fillets in the liquid for 7 minutes. Reserve and keep warm.

Reduce the liquid by a quarter, then add the sour cream.

Add the tomatoes at the last moment to the garlic and shallots.

Arrange the vegetables on the serving dish. Then lay out the fillets an coat with the sauce.

Turbot with Sorrel

PREPARATION: 20 MINUTES
COOKING TIME: 40 MINUTES

SERVES: 4

INGREDIENTS:
4 turbot fillets
4 oz. sorrel
4 oz. sour cream
9 fl. oz. dry white wine
9 fl. oz. fish stock
2 egg yolks
2 bay leaves - crumbled
olive oil
salt, pepper

Wash the fillets under the faucet. Pat dry with absorbent kitchen paper.

Coat an oven dish with olive oil and arrange the fillets on it. Season with salt and pepper. Add the bay leaves. Pour the wine over the top.

Cook for 20 minutes in a fairly hot oven (375°F). Reserve and keep warm.

In the meantime, select the best leaves of the sorrel and remove the fibrous stalks. Brown over a very low heat in a pan with a little olive oil.

Reduce the fish stock by half. Then, in a double-boiler, beat the stock, sour cream, and egg yolks with a whisk.

Lay a bed of sorrel on the bottom of the serving dish. Place the fillets on top and coat with the sauce.

Shellfish

187

Prawns with Green Peppercorns

PREPARATION: 25 MINUTES
COOKING TIME: 20 MINUTES

SERVES: 4

INGREDIENTS:
1 lb. prawns
3 shallots - sliced
7 fl. oz. dry white wine
2 oz. sour cream
olive oil
2 tablespoons green
  peppercorns

Recommended side dishes: Leek clafoutis
Artichokes provençale

In a large pot over a low heat, fry the shallots in a tablespoon of olive oil until translucent.

Add the white wine and simmer for 2 minutes.

Then add the prawns and cook over a high heat for 5 minutes.

Take out the prawns and reserve on a serving dish.

Add the peppercorns to the cooking juices and reduce by half.

Turn down the heat and add the sour cream. Cook for 2 minutes. Reserve and keep warm.

Peel the prawns. Add the tails to the sauce and heat for 2 to 3 minutes before serving.

Lobster Martinique

PREPARATION: 10 MINUTES
COOKING TIME: 25 MINUTES

SERVES: 4

INGREDIENTS:

2 lobsters weighing 1 to
  1½ lb.

3¼ lb. tomatoes

12 cloves garlic - crushed

4 tablespoons olive oil

2 tablespoons freshly
  chopped parsley

½ glass rum

salt, freshly ground
  pepper

Recommended side dishes: Skewered vegetables
provençale
Tomato flan

Blanch to tomatoes in boiling water for 30 seconds. Peel and remove the seeds.

Heat the olive oil in a large casserole. Add the lobsters, cook for 10 minutes turning frequently.

Pour the rum into the casserole and flambé.

Add the garlic. Then, after a couple of minutes, add the tomatoes and the parsley.

Reduce the heat, cover and simmer gently for 15 minutes.

Mussels with Soy Cream

PREPARATION: 10 MINUTES
COOKING TIME: 20 MINUTES

SERVES: 4

INGREDIENTS:
4½ lb. cleaned mussels
6 shallots - finely sliced
7 fl. oz. dry white wine
14 fl. oz. soy cream
olive oil
sea salt, freshly ground
   pepper
Herbs de Provence

Clean the mussels in several changes of water. Remove their beards. Immerse in a large pan of fresh water. Throw away those mussels that rise to the surface, are broken, or do not close when tapped.

In a large pan, brown the shallots in 3 tablespoons olive oil over a low heat. Season the boil and cook for 2 minutes.

Pour the mussels into the large pan and cover. Turn the heat to maximum. Cook for approximately 5 minutes, stirring frequently. Shake the pan a few times until the mussels have opened.

Turn the heat down so the mussels barely simmer. Add the cream of soy and stir. Cover and cook for 1 minute.

Serve with a ladle into soup plates.

190

Poached Oysters on a Bed of Leeks

PREPARATION: 20 MINUTES
COOKING TIME: 25 MINUTES

SERVES: 4

INGREDIENTS:
2 dozen medium oysters
3 leek whites
3 tablespoons sour cream
3 shallots - sliced
1 glass dry white wine
olive oil
salt, freshly ground
    pepper

In a casserole, brown the shallots with 1 tablespoon of olive oil. Add the white wine. Season with salt and pepper. Reduce by a third and reserve.

Clean the leeks. Cut each leek into 2 or 3 sections and then slice down their length into julienne strips. Fry over a low heat in olive oil. Cover and sweat. Reserve and keep warm.

Open the oysters (use a steel glove and special knife if possible, to avoid the risk of injury). Detach them from their shells and conserve half the liquid, adding it to the wine mixture.

Place the casserole over a medium heat and poach the oysters for 2 minutes. Remove them with a slotted spoon, reserve and keep warm.

Reduce the cooking juices to a quarter. Turn down the heat and add the sour cream. Season with pepper.

Lay a bed of leeks on each individual plate and arrange the oysters on top, coating with the sauce.

Serve immediately.

Scallops with Shallots and Cream of Soy

PREPARATION: 5 MINUTES
COOKING TIME: 10 MINUTES

SERVES: 4

INGREDIENTS:
16 scallops
8 shallots - sliced
5 fl. oz. dry white wine
4 tablespoons olive oil
7 fl. oz. cream of soy
2 teaspoons Herbs de
    Provence
salt, freshly ground
    pepper, cayenne

Recommended side dishes: Braised leeks
                         Broccoli
                         Extra fine French beans

Fry the shallots over a gentle heat, stirring occasionally for 5 minutes until they are translucent.

Season with salt, pepper, and cayenne. Sprinkle with Herbs de Provence.

Add the scallops. Raise the heat slightly and brown for 1 minute on each side. Slowly add the wine. Stir and leave to simmer for 1 minute.

Add the soy cream. Allow to simmer for a further minute.

Serve immediately.

192

Side Dishes

Having decided on the main dish for the meal, the cook is then left with the problem of deciding which side dish to choose.

For various reasons, there is a natural tendency to produce what is quickly prepared and what is familiar. As a result, the cook tends to produce the same old dishes time and again. This is a pity, because the variety of vegetables available to us throughout the year, is greater than it has ever been.

For this reason, many of the main dishes in this book suggest side dishes to accompany them.

A significant number of these dishes feature as recipes in this section. They cover a wide selection of vegetables and range from the simple and traditional, to the more elaborate Gratin dishes, which can stand on their own as a light meal, eaten perhaps with a salad.

Vegetables are of course delicious when steamed, then dressed with olive oil or a vinaigrette. Steamed for about 20 minutes they will not only be tender, they will also be highly nutritious. For someone looking for convenience, a small electric steamer is an excellent investment and not expensive.

Vegetables particularly suited for cooking this way, are:
Asparagus, Broad Beans, Small Broad Beans, Broccoli, Brussel Sprouts, Cabbage, Celeriac, Chicory, Cauliflower, Eggplants, Fennel, French Beans, Leeks, Mushrooms, Peppers, Petite Peas, Salsify, Spinach, Sweet Peas, Tomatoes, and Zucchinis.

Artichokes Provençale

PREPARATION: 15 MINUTES
COOKING TIME: 2 HOURS

SERVES: 4

INGREDIENTS:
8 artichokes
3 onions - sliced
3 cloves garlic - crushed
3 tablespoons olive oil
1 sprig thyme
3 bay leaves
salt, freshly ground
    pepper

Remove the hard outer leaves of the artichokes and cut the remainder down to the heart. Cook for 30 minutes in boiling salted water. Put the water to one side.

In a casserole, heat the olive oil and fry the onions over a gentle heat. Add the garlic in the last minutes. Season with salt and pepper.

Add the artichokes, thyme and bay leaves. Cover with the hot water put on one side. Allow to boil gently for about 1 hour 30 minutes.

Eggplant Gratin with Tomato

PREPARATION: 20 MINUTES
COOKING TIME: 55 MINUTES

SERVES: 4-5

INGREDIENTS:
2¼ lb. eggplants
1 lb. tomato sauce
(Recipe no.2)
1 lb. tomatoes, blanched,
skinned, de-seeded
and diced
4 cloves garlic - crushed
1 tablespoon Herbs de
Provence
2 tablespoons olive oil
2 tablespoons freshly
chopped basil
4 cloves garlic
7 oz. grated Gruyére
cheese
7 oz. Mozzarella cheese -
sliced
olive oil
Herbs de Provence
2 tablespoons freshly
chopped basil
salt, freshly ground
pepper

This dish may be served hot, lukewarm, or even cold. It can also be served as a starter.

Cut the eggplants down their length into slices ½ in. thick. Cook in a steamer for 15 to 20 minutes. Allow to drain for a few moments.

Prepare the tomato sauce (see below).

Brush olive oil onto an ovenware dish. Arrange the sliced eggplants over the bottom.

Spread some of the sauce liberally over the top and sprinkle with grated Gruyére. Arrange another layer of eggplant slices over the top. Coat again with tomato sauce and sprinkle with grated Gruyére cheese. Continue until the supply of eggplant slices is exhausted.

With the final layer of sauce, cover with Mozzarella cheese slices ¼ in. thick and sprinkle with Herbs de Provence.

Place in a pre-heated oven (320°F) for 35 minutes. Serve either hot, lukewarm or cold.

To make the sauce (coulis):

Pour boiling water over the tomatoes. After 30 seconds, pour off the water and peel the tomatoes. Remove the seeds and dice the flesh. Place in a liquidizer.

Add the crushed garlic, 1 tablespoon Herbs de Provence, 2 tablespoons olive oil. And 2 tablespoons of freshly basil. Liquefy into a purée.

V

Braised Chicory

PREPARATION: 5 MINUTES
COOKING TIME: 1 HOUR 10 MINUTES

SERVES: 4

INGREDIENTS:
8 heads of chicory
olive oil
salt, freshly ground
  pepper

Cook the chicory in boiling salted water for 50 minutes. Drain well.

Cut in half and fry the chicory in olive oil for 10 to 15 minutes.

Season with salt and pepper.

Serve.

Braised Fennel

PREPARATION: 5 MINUTES
COOKING TIME: 1 HOUR 15 MINUTES

SERVES: 4

INGREDIENTS:
4 fennel heads
olive oil
salt, freshly ground
    pepper

Cook the fennel for 60 minutes in boiling salted water. Drain well.

Heat 3 tablespoons of olive oil in a pan. Add the fennel and cook over a gentle heat for 15 minutes, turning regularly. Season with salt and pepper.

Braised Leeks

PREPARATION: 10 MINUTES
COOKING TIME: 40 MINUTES

SERVES: 4

INGREDIENTS:
2¼ lb. leeks
olive oil

Remove the roots of the leeks. Remove the green part of stem 1 in. below the point where it changes color. Throw away the outer leaves and ensure there is no sand embedded in the plant. Wash and drain.

Chop the leeks into 1 in. lengths.

Heat gently 3 tablespoons of olive oil in a large pan. Then add the leeks. Stir well, cover and simmer for about 35 minutes. Occasionally remove the lid to stir. Season with salt and pepper.

Check to see whether the leeks are properly cooked.

When very tender, remove from the heat and serve on a warm plate.

Broccoli Purée with Soy Cream

PREPARATION: 5 MINUTES
COOKING TIME: 25 MINUTES

SERVES: 4

INGREDIENTS:
1¾ lb. broccoli
7 fl. oz. soy cream
salt, freshly ground
    pepper

Cook the broccoli for 25 minutes in a steamer.

Transfer to a bowl. Season with salt and pepper, then add the soy cream and stir together thoroughly.

Crush with a fork or purée in a food processor.

Serve in a warm dish.

Brussels Sprouts from Gers

PREPARATION: 10 MINUTES
COOKING TIME: 20 MINUTES

SERVES: 4

INGREDIENTS:
2¼ lb. Brussels sprouts
2 cubes beef bouillon
goose fat
freshly ground pepper
nutmeg

Clean and wash the sprouts.

Bring 6 to 8 pints of water to the boil. Dissolve 2 bouillon cubes in the boiling water and season with pepper.

Add the sprouts. When the water has come back to the boil, lower the heat. Allow to boil gently for about 12 minutes.

Drain the sprouts.

In a frying pan or wok, melt 2 tablespoons goose fat over a medium heat. Add the sprouts and sauté until lightly browned.

Transfer to a warm shallow dish and grate a little nutmeg on the top and serve.

Cauliflower Gratin

PREPARATION: 15 MINUTES
COOKING TIME: 30 MINUTES

SERVES: 5

INGREDIENTS:
1 large cauliflower -
  between 2¼ - 3 lb.
9 oz. grated Gruyére
  cheese
14 fl. oz. light cream
salt, freshly ground
  pepper

This dish may also be served as a starter or main dish.

Wash the cauliflower. Cut the florets from the stem and cook for 15 minutes in a large pan of salted, boiling water. Drain well.

In a bowl, mix the grated Gruyére and the light cream. Season generously with pepper.

Oil a shallow oven dish. Arrange the florets and pour the cream mixture over the top.

Place under a well-heated broiler for 10 to 12 minutes.

Serve very hot in the shallow oven dish.

Celeriac Purée

PREPARATION: 10 MINUTES
COOKING TIME: 1 HOUR 15 MINUTES

SERVES: 4

INGREDIENTS:
1 celeriac
1 lemon
10 fl. oz. light cream
salt, freshly ground
    pepper, nutmeg

Peel and wash the celeriac.

Cut into large cubes. Cook for an hour in boiling salted water together with the lemon which has been cut into quarters.

Drain the celeriac and discard the pieces of lemon.

Add the cream to the celeriac. Season with salt and pepper. Sprinkle with the grated nutmeg.

Simmer over a very gentle heat, until the cream has been absorbed by the celeriac. Transfer to the blender and make into a purée.

Adjust the seasoning and serve on a warm dish.

Crushed Olives with Capers and Anchovies

PREPARATION: 10 MINUTES
NO COOKING

**THIS RECIPE
MAKES 28 OZ.
OF TAPENADE.**

INGREDIENTS:
9 oz. pitted black olives

4 oz. anchovy fillets

4 oz. tuna in olive oil

8 oz. capers

1 tablespoon Dijon
    Mustard

1 glass brandy - 2 fl. oz.

7 fl. oz. olive oil

salt, freshly ground
    pepper, paprika

This dish should be stored in a large sealed jar and kept in the refrigerator. It can be used with may other dishes or just simply as a spread on toast made from 'integral bread' - bread made with unrefined flour.

Put all the ingredients into a blender and reduce to a paste.

Cured Ham with Zucchinis and Parmesan

PREPARATION: 15 MINUTES
COOKING TIME: 20 MINUTES

SERVES: 4

INGREDIENTS:
8 slices of cured ham
4 nice zucchinis
4 large tomatoes
4 oz. grated Parmesan
   cheese
olive oil
chopped parsley
salt, freshly ground
   pepper

To make this into a main dish, just add a couple of large free-range eggs fried in goose fat.

Dice the zucchinis.

Pour boiling water over the tomatoes for 30 seconds. Drain, peel, and remove the seeds. Dice the tomato flesh.

Fry the zucchinis and the tomatoes over a medium heat for about 12 minutes, stirring frequently. Season with salt and pepper.

Gradually add the grated Parmesan to the pan, together with another tablespoon of olive oil.

Cook over a low heat for 5 to 6 minutes, stirring occasionally.

Arrange the slices of ham in individual plates. Serve the zucchinis with the cheese mixture on top. Sprinkle with chopped parsley.

Farmhouse Quiche

PREPARATION: 15 MINUTES
COOKING TIME: 1 HOUR 10 MINUTES

SERVES: 4-5

INGREDIENTS:
5 eggs
1¼ lb. leeks
5 oz. diced marbled bacon
1 large onion - sliced
10 oz. low-fat sour cream
7 oz. grated Gouda cheese
olive oil
salt, freshly ground pepper, nutmeg

This dish may also be served as a main dish with salad, or as a starter.

Wash the leeks and discard the thick green parts. Cut into slices ½ in. thick.

Fry the diced marbled bacon in a large frying pan over a gentle heat, to extract as much fat as possible. Reserve and keep warm.

In a casserole, heat 2 tablespoons of olive oil. Add the onion and leeks and cook over a low heat. Stir well. Cook slowly for 20 minutes, stirring from time to time. Season with salt and pepper.

Break the eggs into a bowl. Beat together with the sour cream. Add a little salt, pepper, and freshly grated nutmeg. Add the grated cheese and mix well.

Using the slotted spoon, remove the diced marbled bacon, onions and leeks from their respective pans and transfer to the bowl containing the egg and sour cream mixture. Mix well.

Pour the preparation into 11 in. flan dish that has been brushed with olive oil. Cook in a double-boiler in a warm oven (320°F) for 40 minutes.

Serve lukewarm.

206

Fresh Tomatoes with Spicy Filling

PREPARATION: 20 MINUTES
NO COOKING

SERVES: 4

INGREDIENTS:
5-6 tomatoes
7 oz. tuna in brine
2 oz. anchovy fillets
2 oz. capers
2 oz. gherkins
1 egg yolk
1 teaspoon mustard
olive oil
2 cloves garlic
salt, freshly ground
   pepper, paprika

Grate the cloves of garlic.

Dice the gherkins very finely.

Make a small amount of mayonnaise with the egg yolk, the teaspoon of mustard and the olive oil.

Blend the tuna, anchovy fillets, and capers in a food processor. Mix with the mayonnaise, grated garlic, and chopped gherkin, into a creamy mixture. Add a little olive oil if necessary.

Adjust the seasoning with salt, pepper, and paprika. The salpicon stuffing is now ready.

Cut off the tops of the tomatoes, hollow them out with a small spoon and stuff with the salpicon.

Arrange on a dish or on individual plates and leave in a cool place for 2 to 3 hours before serving.

Leek Clafoutis

PREPARATION: 15 MINUTES
COOKING TIME: 1 HOUR 10 MINUTES

SERVES: 4

INGREDIENTS:
5 good-sized leeks
10 oz. cottage cheese
3 whole eggs + 1 yolk
1 clove garlic - crushed
    with a little ginger
4 oz. Gruyère cheese
salt, freshly ground
    pepper

This dish may also be served as a starter or as a main dish in a light meal.

Prepare the leeks. Cut the white part of the leek into sections 1 in. long. Cook in a steamer for 20 minutes. Drain well.

In a bowl, beat the eggs with the yolk and then add the cottage cheese, stirring in well. Then stir in the Gruyère cheese and the crushed garlic and ginger.

Arrange the leeks in the bottom of an oiled 11 in. ovenware dish. Pour the egg mixture on top.

Put in a very cool oven and bake for 45 minutes (200°F).

Sprinkle the rest of the Gruyère cheese over the top of the dish and broil for a few minutes, until the cheese turns crunchy.

Onion Gratin

PREPARATION: 15 MINUTES
COOKING TIME: 55 MINUTES

SERVES: 5

INGREDIENTS:
1¼ lb. onions - sliced
5 oz. sour cream
6 eggs
4 oz. grated Gruyère cheese
4 oz. Mozzarella cheese - thinly sliced
olive oil
salt, freshly ground pepper

Fry the onions in a large frying pan in 3 tablespoons olive oil over a gentle heat, stirring continuously. Cook until most of their moisture has evaporated and the onions are golden brown. Season with salt and pepper.

In a large bowl, beat together the eggs, grated cheese, and sour cream. Season sparingly with salt and pepper. Using a slotted spoon, transfer the onions from pan to bowl. Stir until completely mixed.

Pour the mixture into a shallow oven dish and cook for 40 minutes in the oven (250°F).

Slice the Mozzarella as finely as possible, and cover the dish with the slices.

Place the dish under the broiler until the cheese melts.

Parsley Mushrooms

PREPARATION: 20 MINUTES
COOKING TIME: 15 MINUTES

SERVES: 4

INGREDIENTS:
1¾ lb. fairly large button
  mushrooms
6 cloves garlic - sliced
2 tablespoons freshly
  chopped parsley
olive oil
salt, freshly ground
  pepper

This dish may also be used as a starter.

Remove the base of the stalks. Wash and wipe clean. Drain well. Slice lengthwise.

Heat 3 tablespoons olive oil in a frying pan over a gentle heat. Fry the mushrooms and stir well with a wooden spoon.

When the mushrooms have lost their water, throw away the cooking juices and add a further 3 tablespoons of olive oil. Season with salt and pepper. Stir for about 1 minute over a low heat.

Scrape the mushrooms to the side, then tilt the pan so that all the cooking oil drains to the empty part. In the oily part of the pan, brown the crushed garlic and the chopped parsley, then mix well with the mushrooms.

Serve immediately.

Ratatouille

PREPARATION: 20 MINUTES
COOKING TIME: 60 MINUTES

SERVES: 5-6

INGREDIENTS:
3 good-sized eggplants
3 red peppers
2¼ lb. tomatoes - skinned
3 zucchinis
3 onions
4 cloves garlic
Herbs de Provence
olive oil
salt, freshly ground pepper, cayenne

This dish is even better when reheated after being allowed to stand.

Halve the red peppers down their length. Remove the stalk and the seeds. Place under the grill skin side up until slightly charred. Allow to cool and remove the skin. Cut into strips.

Cut the eggplants into thick 1 in. cubes.

Over a gentle heat, fry in a casserole or a wok some olive oil for 30 minutes. Stir regularly.

Cut the zucchinis into large dice and fry in olive oil. Stir regularly.

Cut the tomatoes into pieces and cook in an open casserole with some olive oil, until they have lost their liquid.

Fry the onions and the garlic over a very gentle heat in some olive oil.

Put all the vegetables without their cooking juices in a large pan.

Pour about 5 fl. oz. olive oil over the top. Sprinkle with Herbs de Provence.

Season with salt, pepper, and a pinch of cayenne pepper.

Stir well and simmer with no cover for 15 minutes over a very low heat.

Serve either hot or cold.

Skewered Vegetables Provençale

PREPARATION: 20 MINUTES
COOKING TIME: 15-20 MINUTES

SERVES: 4

INGREDIENTS:
8 small firm tomatoes
4 large button
   mushrooms
2 large onions
2 red peppers
olive oil
salt, freshly ground
   pepper, Herbs de
   Provence

Cut the tomatoes in half and the onions and mushrooms into quarters.

Cut the peppers in half. Remove the stem and the seeds, then cut into 1 in. squares.

To make up a skewer, thread ½ tomato, ¼ onion, a square of pepper, ¼ mushroom, ½ tomato, and so on - completing the row with ½ tomato.

Brush with olive oil. Season with salt and pepper. Sprinkle with Herbs de Provence.

Arrange the skewers on an oven pan and place the pan about 4 in. below the broiler.

Grill, turning the skewer regularly a turn at a time.

Spinach with Soy Cream

PREPARATION: 15 MINUTES
COOKING TIME: 45 MINUTES

SERVES: 4

INGREDIENTS:
4½ lb. spinach
2 tablespoons goose fat
1 bunch of parsley
7 fl. oz. soy cream
salt, freshly ground
   pepper

Wash the spinach and remove the stalks. Drain.

In a casserole, melt 2 tablespoons of goose fat. Then add the spinach.

Cover and allow to cook for 12 minutes over a very gentle heat. Season with salt and add the bunch of parsley. Stir.

Cove again and leave to cook for 30 minutes.

Transfer the spinach to a food processor and add the soy cream. Blend.

Return to the pan and warm the vegetable mixture gently, for no more than a minute to prevent the soy cream from coagulating.

Season with salt and pepper.

213

Tagliatelle with Pesto

PREPARATION: 15 MINUTES
COOKING TIME: 10 MINUTES

SERVES: 4-5

INGREDIENTS:
1 lb. tagliatelle made
   from unrefined flour
4 cloves garlic - crushed
9 oz. grated Parmesan
   cheese
15 leaves basil
7 tablespoons olive oil
3 oz. pine nuts
salt, freshly ground
   pepper

This dish makes a good starter or main dish for a light meal.

Boil salted water in a tall large pan. Add 1 teaspoon of olive oil.

Crush the garlic and chopped basil leaves together in a mortar, until a paste is formed. Add olive oil little by little and mix together with a wooden spoon. Then add the grated Parmesan cheese. (Alternatively, put all the ingredients in a food processor and blend.) Season very light with salt and pepper.

When the water is bubbling fiercely, add the tagliatelli. Cook until 'al dente' - between 6 to 12 minutes, depending on the make.

When the tagliatelli are cooked, turn off the heat and add a cupful of cold water to the pan to arrest further cooking. Drain in a colander and serve in individual plates.

Top with the sauce and add the pine nuts.

214

Tomato Flan

PREPARATION: 15 MINUTES
COOKING TIME: 55 MINUTES

SERVES: 4-5

INGREDIENTS:
8 to 10 tomatoes
   (depending on size)
5 eggs + 1 yolk
7 fl. oz. light cream
5 oz. grated Gruyère
   cheese
4 oz. Mozzarella - finely
   sliced
1 tablespoon of freshly
   chopped basil

This dish can also be served as a starter or as a main dish.

Cover the tomatoes with boiling water for 30 seconds. Peel and remove the seeds.

Dice the flesh and drain for a good 30 minutes, to ensure they lose as much water as possible.

Melt the grated Gruyère in the light cream over a gentle heat and stir continuously with a wooden spoon.

Arrange the diced tomatoes evenly in an oiled 11 in. ovenware flan dish.

Beat the eggs and yolk, the creamed Gruyère, and the basil. Season generously with salt and pepper. Pour over the diced tomatoes in the earthenware dish.

Bake in a very cool oven (250°F) for 40 minutes.

Before serving, spread the slice of Mozzarella on top of the dish. Place under the broiler for a few minutes.

Traditional Cabbage

PREPARATION: 15 MINUTES
COOKING TIME: 2 HOURS 20 MINUTES

SERVES: 5-6

INGREDIENTS:
1 large cabbage - about
   3¼ lb.
9 oz. marbled bacon
2 onions - sliced
bouquet garni (bay,
   thyme and parsley)
2 beef bouillon cubes
goose fat
salt, freshly ground
   pepper

The liquid produced during the cooking may be retained to make a soup, by liquefying with the remainder of the cabbage.

Heat a large pan full of salted water. Remove the outer leaves of the cabbage. Quarter. Remove the stem and the larger stalks.

Blanch for 20 minutes. Drain well.

In a large casserole, melt 1 tablespoon goose fat and gently fry the diced marbled bacon over a low heat. Then add the sliced onions and fry until golden brown.

Add the cabbage leaves, bouquet garni and crumble the bouillon cubes over the top. Cover with water. Season lightly with pepper and salt.

Cover and boil gently for 2 hours.

Turn out onto a shallow dish, remove the bouquet garni, then serve.

216

Salads

To make a good salad, it is essential all the ingredients should be as fresh as possible and of the best quality.

The seasoning should include salt. Vinegar is also an essential ingredient: it should be made from red wine. And it need not be expensive, for it is quite easily made at home. Stoneware pots with a wooden tap made specifically for the purpose are easily obtainable. All you need to do is soak the wooden tap well before inserting it in the pot with its bung, pour in a bottle of wine and add the culture. From then on, just add all your wine remains - white or red - and keep the pot in the cool.

Sherry vinegar is often used for de-glazing the cooking pan, but its distinctive flavor gives added character to a salad.

Balsamic vinegar, with its very particular character, is generally used cut with ordinary wine vinegar to make its effect more subtle.

Another very important ingredient in a dressing, is mustard. There are many different types, but the one most used in France is Moutarde Forte de Dijon.

Then of course, we have the vegetable oils. Three main types are used normally:

SUNFLOWER OIL, which had to be purified to make its very strong flavor more acceptable.

OLIVE OIL, which should state on its label that it is Virgin and that it is from the First Cold Pressing. When it fulfills these two conditions, olive oil is the queen of oils and should be used in abundance, because it is very good for you.

WALNUT OIL, which is very aromatic, makes a remarkable difference to a salad. The only drawback to its use is that it does not keep very long, once the bottle is opened. To prevent it from becoming rancid relatively quickly, it must be refrigerated. For this reason, it is advisable to purchase it only in small amounts - 9 to 18 fl. oz.

Mixed herbs are not essential but they are always welcome. The classic herbs are parsley, tarragon, basil and chives.

When we think of spices, the first one that comes to mind is pepper, either freshly ground or crushed in a pestle to conserve its wonderful aroma. However, there are others that make a valuable contribution to a vinaigrette. A discreet pinch of curry powder gives an added sense of character, and you can afford to be rather more generous with mild paprika.

And then last - but by no means least - we have garlic and Herbs de Provence. To those that come from the South East of France, they are indispensable elements in any salad and as far as garlic is concerned, extremely good for you. However, those that find it too pungent can always use it more sparingly - just enough to give their vinaigrette that little air of mystery.

Improvised Salads

Here are a few ideas for salads that are normally improvised according to the ingredients that happen to be available at the time.

PHASE 1:

Artichoke and asparagus salad

Avocado salad, tomatoes, tuna, hard-boiled eggs, Gruyère cheese, lettuce

Cucumber and tomato salad

Curly endive salad with diced bacon

Endive salad with Roquefort cheese or walnuts

French bean and smoked salmon salad

Fresh spinach salad, with walnuts and Gruyère cheese

Green salad (lettuce, lamb's lettuce, watercress, dandelion, lollo rosso, lollo biondo, oakleaf lettuce, cos, frisée, etc.), plain or mixed, with or without herbs, but always with a good vinaigrette.

Green salad, extra-thin French beans, tomatoes

Green salad with warm goat's cheese

Palm heart salad

Tomatoes, basil, goat's cheese (or feta)

PHASE 2:

Lentil salad with shallots (the shallots should be sliced very thinly and the vinaigrette should have a generous dose of mustard)

Chickpea salad with a pinch of cumin

Red kidney bean salad with a pinch of ground coriander and a generous sprinkling of olive oil

Asparagus Salad with Smoked Salmon

PREPARATION: 20 MINUTES
COOKING TIME: 50 MINUTES

SERVES: 4

INGREDIENTS:
1¾ lb. asparagus
7 oz. smoked salmon -
   thinly sliced
4 sprigs dill - chopped
4 slices lemon
7 fl. oz. whipping cream
1½ tablespoon strong
   Dijon mustard

Wash and peel the asparagus. Cook in salted water for about 20 minutes or until tender (test with the point of a knife). Drain well.

Whip the cream until stiff. Stir in the mustard and chopped dill.

Roll the salmon slices around the asparagus near their tips.

Arrange the asparagus attractively on a rectangular dish.

Coat them with the sauce and decorate with the dill and lemon slices.

Avocado Salad with Peppers

PREPARATION: 15 MINUTES
COOKING TIME: 15 TO 20 MINUTES

SERVES: 4

INGREDIENTS:
2 ripe avocados
2 red peppers
4 chicory heads
a few leaves assorted
   lettuce
2 tablespoons chopped
   parsley
20 black olives - stones
   removed
vinaigrette provençale
   (see page 194)
lemon

Put the red peppers in a pre-heated oven (400°F) and bake for 20 minutes until the skin blisters. Cool and peel the skin. Cut the flesh into thin strips.

Halve the avocados lengthways, stone, peel and slice. Sprinkle with lemon juice to prevent them from going brown. Remove the pits from the olives and chop.

Prepare the assorted lettuce leaves.

Cut the chicory into slices (¼ in.) thick.

To serve, arrange the lettuce, avocado, chicory, and red peppers on individual plates. Pour the vinaigrette on the top and sprinkle with parsley and chopped olives.

Bacon and Broad Bean Salad

PREPARATION: 20 MINUTES
COOKING TIME: 25 MINUTES

SERVES: 4

INGREDIENTS:
3¼ lb. fresh broad beans
5 oz. bacon
1 onion
1 bunch fresh mint
5 fl. oz. olive oil
1 tablespoon balsamic
   vinegar
salt, freshly ground
   pepper

Shell the beans and cook for 15 to 20 minutes in a large pan of salted water. Drain, allow to cool and remove the fine membrane that covers the bean by pinching it between thumb and index finger.

Peek, halve and slice the onion.

Chop about ten leaves of mint very finely.

Cut the slices of bacon into 4 and brown in a non-stick pan with a little olive oil and the sliced onion.

Make the vinaigrette in a bowl: add salt and pepper to the balsamic vinegar, then add the olive oil and mix vigorously.

Add the beans, bacon, onion, and mint. Toss and serve on individual plates. Decorate with the rest of the mint leaves and serve.

V

Broccoli Salad with Almonds

PREPARATION: 15 MINUTES
COOKING TIME: 15 MINUTES

SERVES: 4

INGREDIENTS:
1 lb. broccoli
3 oz. almonds
2 red peppers
2 tablespoons chopped
  parsley
vinaigrette provençale
  (see page 194)

Put the red peppers into a pre-heated oven (400°F) or steamer until blistered. Cool and peel. Cut into thin strips.

Divide the broccoli into florets and cook in a steamer for 15 minutes. Allow to cool.

On individual plates, arrange the broccoli with almonds and strips of red pepper on the top.

Pour the vinaigrette over the dish and sprinkle with chopped parsley.

Celeriac and Avocado Remoulade

PREPARATION: 20 MINUTES
NO COOKING

SERVES: 4

INGREDIENTS:
1 large celeriac weighing about 1¼ lb.
1 ripe avocado
8 oz. yogurt
1 dozen black olives - stones removed
1 lemon
1 tablespoon strong mustard
3 tablespoons olive oil
2 cloves garlic
1 tablespoon powdered wheat germ
1 tablespoon chopped parsley
salt, freshly ground pepper, ground coriander

Peel the celeriac, cut into manageable pieces and grate. Sprinkle lemon juice over the top to prevent it from oxidizing and going brown.

Crush the garlic. Remove the stone from the avocado and scoop out the flesh.

To make the sauce:

Put the avocado, yogurt, mustard, wheat germ, olive oil, garlic, and black olives into a food processor. Season with salt and pepper. Add a few pinches of coriander and blend for a few seconds to obtain a sauce with the consistency of a mayonnaise.

Mix the celeriac with the sauce.

Arrange in a serving dish or on individual plates, and decorate with chopped parsley.

Chicken Salad

PREPARATION: 20 MINUTES
COOKING TIME: 20 MINUTES

SERVES: 4

INGREDIENTS:
1 small head of lettuce
4 stalks celery
4 boneless chicken breasts
4 hard-boiled eggs
24 black olives - stones removed
24 green olives, stones removed
sweet paprika
salt, freshly ground pepper, vinaigrette and/or mayonnaise
goose fat

This dish may be served either with vinaigrette or with mayonnaise.

Cook the chicken in goose fat for no more than 20 minutes over a very low heat. Season with salt and pepper. Allow to cool and cut into slices 1 in. thick.

Take the best leaves of the lettuce and cut into strips.

Chop the celery stalks into small pieces.

Cut the hard-boiled eggs into slices and sprinkle with paprika.

Dress the individual plates with lettuce, chicken, celery, eggs, and olives.

Serve with vinaigrette or mayonnaise.

225

Dandelion Salad with Bacon and Cheese

PREPARATION: 20 MINUTES
COOKING TIME: 5 MINUTES

SERVES: 4

INGREDIENTS:
¾ lb dandelion leaves
    (or rocket if preferred)
8 oz. Beaufort cheese
5 oz. smoked bacon
2 hard-boiled eggs
1 clove garlic - crushed
12 green olives - stones
    removed
olive oil vinaigrette
salt, freshly ground
    pepper, walnut oil

Clean and wash the dandelion leaves in 3 changes of water. Drain well.

Dice the smoked bacon and blanch for 4 minutes in unsalted boiling water. Drain and pat dry with absorbent kitchen paper. Fry over a gentle heat in a non-stick frying pan until crisp.

Prepare the vinaigrette: dissolve the salt in the vinegar. Add the crushed garlic, pepper, and olive oil. Mix well.

Cut the Beaufort cheese into cubes and slice the hard-boiled eggs.

Place the dandelion leaves in large bowl and add the warm diced bacon, cheese, and eggs. Toss in the vinaigrette. Add the olives and lace with walnut oil before serving.

French Vinaigrette

PREPARATION IN A BOTTLE OR CRUET

INGREDIENTS:
1 tablespoon strong mustard
5 fl. oz. wine vinegar
7 fl. oz. sunflower oil
7 fl. oz. olive oil
1 teaspoon sea salt
3 grindings of pepper
1 clove garlic - crushed
1 teaspoon Herbs de Provence
3 pinches mild paprika
1 small pinch cayenne
1 pinch curry powder

Dissolve all the solid ingredients in the vinegar. Add the oils and shake well.

Vinaigrette Provençale: Is very similar to this general recipe. However, it contains only olive oil - 14 fl. oz.

227

Gourmand Salad

PREPARATION: 25 MINUTES
COOKING TIME: 55 MINUTES

SERVES: 4

INGREDIENTS:
1 lb. very fine french beans
8 scallops
7 oz. goose liver
1 bunch parsley
balsamic vinaigrette with olive oil
sea salt, freshly ground pepper

If you cannot use fresh goose liver, then use the canned version. Cut into 8 thin slices and arrange on a plate. Cover with plastic film and refrigerate for at least an hour.

Cook the french beans so they remain 'al dente' or slightly firm.

Prepare the vinaigrette: dissolve the salt in the balsamic vinegar and add the pepper and olive oil. Mix well.

Poach the scallops for 5 minutes in water with sea salt and pepper. Drain and reserve.

Just before serving, using a very sharp knife slice the scallops very thinly.

Arrange the french beans edged with the sliced scallops in each plate, and then add the 2 slices of goose liver.

Decorate with parsley and lace with the vinaigrette.

228

Mushroom Salad

PREPARATION: 20 MINUTES
COOKING TIME: 5 MINUTES

SERVES: 4-5

INGREDIENTS:
1 lb. button mushrooms
1 egg yolk
1 glass olive oil
2 lemons
salt, pepper, mustard
1 bunch parsley

Clean the mushrooms well.

In a large pan, add salt and the juice of 1 lemon to 1½ pints of water and bring to the boil. Add the mushrooms and cook for 3 or 4 minutes. Drain well and allow to cool.

To make the mayonnaise, whisk together an egg yolk with 1 teaspoon of mustard and then gradually add the olive oil, beating all the time. Season with salt and pepper and then gradually beat in the juice of the second lemon. Reserve in the fridge.

Slice the mushrooms lengthwise. Add to the mayonnaise and mix well. Sprinkle with chopped parsley and serve.

Red Bean Salad

PREPARATION: 20 MINUTES
COOKING TIME: 1 HOUR 30 MINUTES

SERVES: 4

INGREDIENTS:
8 oz. red beans
8 oz. button mushrooms
4 oz. bean sprouts
2 red peppers
3 tablespoons chopped
   basil
3 tablespoons chopped
   parsley
vinaigrette provençale
walnut oil

Soak the beans for 12 hours in plenty of water. Cook for 1 hour and 15 minutes in slightly salted water.

Clean the button mushrooms. Slice lengthwise and sprinkle with lemon juice to prevent them from turning black.

Put the peppers in a preheated oven (400°F) or steamer for 20 minutes until they blister. Cool, peel and cut into narrow slices.

Put the beans, mushrooms, beans sprouts, red pepper, basil, and parsley into a bowl or into individual plates.

Add a little walnut oil to the vinaigrette, pour over the top and serve.

Red Cabbage Salad with Walnuts

PREPARATION: 15 MINUTES
NO COOKING

SERVES: 5

INGREDIENTS:
1 small red cabbage
1 onion - thinly sliced
2 tablespoons olive oil
2 tablespoons red wine
   vinegar
2 teaspoons walnut oil
1 teaspoon mustard
2 oz. walnuts very
   coarsely chopped
salt, freshly ground
   pepper

Remove the coarse outer leaves of the cabbage. Quarter and slice thinly.

Peel the onion and cut into thin slices. Ensure the slices break up into rings.

Prepare the vinaigrette: dissolve the salt and mustard in the vinegar. Add the pepper, olive oil, and walnut oil. Mix well.

Put the cabbage in a bowl, add the vinaigrette and walnuts. Toss and serve.

Watercress and Bacon Salad

PREPARATION: 15 MINUTES
COOKING TIME: 12 MINUTES

SERVES: 4

INGREDIENTS:
12 oz. watercress
4 oz. marbled bacon
½ glass sherry vinegar
olive oil

Dice the marbled bacon. Blanch for 4 minutes in boiling water. Drain.

Fry the diced marbled bacon in a non-stick pan over a low heat until the fat has melted.

Sort and wash the watercress. Drain and transfer to a large bowl.

Throw away the melted bacon fat and de-glaze the pan with the sherry vinegar. Turn the diced bacon and de-glazing over the watercress. Drizzle olive oil over the top. Toss the salad and serve.

Desserts

Apple Scramble with Cinnamon

PREPARATION: 30 MINUTES
COOKING TIME: 35 MINUTES

SERVES: 4

INGREDIENTS:
8 large ripe apples
3 complete eggs + 3 yolks
4 tablespoons fructose
2 fl. oz. Calvados
6 fl. oz. low-fat sour cream
cinnamon powder

Peel the apples. Quarter and remove the core. Cook in the steamer for about 20 minutes. Drain well.

In a large bowl, beat the egg, yolks, and fructose. Add the apples, Calvados, and sour cream. Sprinkle with cinnamon. Continue to beat with a whisk until the mixture has a uniform consistency.

Pour into a large non-stick pan and cook over a very, very low heat - as for making scrambled eggs - stirring continuously with a spatula. Take the pan off the heat and pour the mixture which should still be slightly moist, into low ovenware dishes or ramekins.

Sprinkle over the top with cinnamon and when quite cool, refrigerate for 2 or 3 hours.

Serve ungarnished or with a chocolate sauce and/or whipped cream.

Apple Soufflé Flambé with Calvados

PREPARATION: 30 MINUTES
COOKING TIME: 55 MINUTES

SERVES: 5

INGREDIENTS:
12 apples
5 egg yolks
5 tablespoons fructose
7 fl. oz. whipping cream
1 teaspoon vanilla
extract
2 fl. oz. Calvados

After this dish has been flamed with Calvados, it can be allowed to cool before browning lightly under a hot broiler.

Peel the apples. Cut into quarters and remove the core.

Brush an ovenware dish lightly with oil and distribute the apple quarters evenly. Sprinkle 2 tablespoons of fructose over the top.

Bake in a very hot oven (450°F) for 25 minutes. Reserve.

In a large bowl, beat the egg yolks with 2 tablespoons of fructose until the mixture begins to turn creamy white.

Whish the cream until very stiff and add 1 tablespoon of fructose.

Pour away the juice that has drained out of the apples. Then mix together well the apples, beaten eggs, whipped cream, and vanilla extract.

Turn into an oiled ovenware dish and cook in a cool oven (250°F) for 35 to 40 minutes. Remove from the oven. Flame with Calvados and serve.

Apricot Bavarois with Sauce

PREPARATION: 20 MINUTES
COOKING TIME: 15 MINUTES

SERVES: 4

INGREDIENTS:
1¾ lb. apricots
5 leaves of gelatin - (or the equivalent of agar-agar)
9 fl. oz. full milk
3½ oz. fructose
7 fl. oz. whipping cream
2 fl. oz. cognac

Cut the apricots in half and remove the stones. Place in a steamer and cook for 10 minutes. Reserve and allow to cool.

Bring the milk to the boil and then allow to cool for 10 minutes.

Immerse the leaves of gelatin in cold water. Squeeze dry and then add to the milk. Stir well and allow to stand for 15 minutes.

Mix 2 oz. of fructose with the cream and beat until stiff.

Fold the whipped cream into the milk (which is just beginning to set) and add the cognac. Stir gently with the whisk to obtain a smooth mixture.

Pour into ramekins or into rings 3 in. in diameter, and refrigerate for 6 hours to allow mixture to set.

To make the sauce (coulis), combine the remaining apricots and fructose in a food processor. Reserve and keep cool.

Un-mold onto individual plates and surround with the sauce.

Apricots and Custard

PREPARATION: 15 MINUTES
COOKING TIME: 20 MINUTES

SERVES: 4

INGREDIENTS:
20 large ripe apricots
2 tablespoons fructose
½ glass rum

For the Custard:
8 egg yolks
1¾ pints milk
3 tablespoons fructose
1 vanilla pod
sugar-free cocoa powder

Split open the apricots and remove the stones.

Place in a steamer skin-side facing downwards. Sprinkle with 2 tablespoons of fructose and cook for 10 minutes. Allow to drain. Flambé with the rum and allow to cool. Reserve in the refrigerator.

Bring the milk with the split vanilla pod slowly to the boil. Remove from the heat and allow to cool for 10 minutes.

Beat the egg yolks, adding the warm milk slowly to the mixture. Then whisk briskly.

Return the mixture to a low heat to thicken (preferably in a double-boiler), beating constantly. When the custard has the right consistency, allow to cool for a few minutes and add fructose.

Refrigerate for several hours.

To serve, place 8 to 10 apricot halves in a shallow dish. Ladle custard over the top and dust with the cocoa powder.

237

Blanc-mange with Raspberry Sauce

PREPARATION: 20 MINUTES
COOKING TIME: 5 MINUTES

SERVES: 5

INGREDIENTS:
8 oz. raspberries
14 oz. cottage cheese - strained
10 oz. whipping cream
4 tablespoons of sugar-free raspberry jam
6 leaves of gelatin (or the equivalent of agar-agar)
1 tablespoon fructose
1 tablespoon rum

Whip the cream until stiff.

Soften the gelatin leaves in cold water. Squeeze dry and dissolve in the rum, which should be slightly warm.

Mix well together the whipped cream, strained cottage cheese, rum, gelatin, and raspberry jam.

Brush the molds with egg white. Arrange some raspberries at the bottom of each mold and pour the rum mixture over the top and place in the refrigerator to set.

Prepare the sauce by liquefying the remaining raspberries with the fructose. Strain through a sieve.

To serve, un-mold the bavarois onto individual plates and coat with the sauce.

Brazilian Mousse

PREPARATION: 20 MINUTES
COOKING TIME: 10 MINUTES

SERVES: 6

INGREDIENTS:
4 tablespoons instant
   coffee
7 fl. oz. whipping cream
6 eggs
3 leaves gelatin (or the
   equivalent of agar-
   agar)
½ glass rum
3½ oz. fructose

In a double-boiler, dissolve the instant coffee in the rum and cream. Add the fructose and dissolve.

Immerse the gelatin in cold water for a few minutes. Remove and squeeze out. Add to the coffee mixture and dissolve. Allow to cool.

Break the eggs and separate the whites from the yolks.

Add a pinch of salt to the whites and whisk until very stiff.

Mix the coffee cream with the egg yolks. Fold the whites carefully into the coffee mixture with a metal spoon.

Refrigerate for 5 to 6 hours.

Before serving, sprinkle with freshly ground coffee beans.

Catalan Cream with Fresh Raspberries

PREPARATION: 15 MINUTES
COOKING TIME: 60 MINUTES

SERVES: 4

INGREDIENTS:
1 container of raspberries
5 egg yolks
12 oz. sour cream
5 fl. oz. full cream milk
3 oz. fructose
1 pinch cinnamon

Bring the milk to the boil and then allow to cool for 10 minutes.

Beat together the egg yolks, fructose, and cinnamon. Whisk until the mixture turns white and creamy.

Stir the milk and sour cream together and then add to the egg mixture, beating continuously.

Cover the bottom of a shallow dish or individual ramekins with raspberries and then pour the final mixture over the top.

Place the shallow dish or ramekins in a hot double-boiler in a pre-heated oven (260°F) and cook for 55 minutes.

Allow to cool to room temperature and refrigerate for at least 4 hours.

Before serving, the catalan cream can be broiled for a few minutes until golden brown.

Cherry Flan

PREPARATION: 15 MINUTES
COOKING TIME: 60 MINUTES

SERVES: 5

INGREDIENTS:
1¾ lb. cherries, stones removed
7 fl. oz. milk
7 fl. oz. whipping cream
2 oz. fructose
6 eggs
6 tablespoons rum
vanilla extract

Soak the cherries in the rum.

Heat the milk and the whipping cream without boiling. Allow to cool.

In a large bowl, beat together the eggs with the fructose. Pour in the milk, stirring constantly. Add a few drops of vanilla extract.

Arrange the cherries in a 11 in. flan dish.

Add the rum from the cherries to the milk mixture and pour over the cherries in the flan.

Cook for 50 minutes in the oven (260°F). Allow to cool before refrigerating. Chill completely before serving.

Chestnut and Chocolate Mousse

PREPARATION: 20 MINUTES
COOKING TIME: 15 MINUTES

SERVES: 5

INGREDIENTS:
3¼ lb. chestnuts
7 oz. chocolate with
   70% cocoa solids
4 oz. sour cream
3 tablespoons fructose
2 fl. oz. milk
1 vanilla pod
3 oz. cognac

Peel the chestnuts. Boil for 5 minutes to ease removal of the inner skin.

Then cook over a low heat in the vanilla milk for about 30 minutes, until soft.

Drain and reduce to a purée using the potato masher.

Melt the chocolate with the cognac in a double-boiler.

In a large bowl, mix the chestnuts, melted chocolate, sour cream and fructose together thoroughly.

Line a mold with aluminum foil which has been lightly greased. Pour in the mixture. Cover with plastic film and refrigerate for at least 5 hours.

Un-mold and serve onto a melted chocolate base coating individual plates. If preferred, decorate also with whipped cream.

Chocolate Truffles

PREPARATION: 20 MINUTES
NO COOKING

THIS RECIPE
MAKES ABOUT
30 TRUFFLES.

INGREDIENTS:
6 oz. unsweetened cocoa
   powder
3 oz. fine fructose
   powder
5 oz. butter - unsalted
2 egg yolks
3 oz. sour cream

Remove the butter from the refrigerator 4 hours before starting the recipe. Do this to ensure the butter is at room temperature when you start working.

Put the butter in a basin and work with a wooden spoon until the texture is completely smooth.

Incorporate first the egg yolks, then the fructose, and then the cocoa. Continue stirring with a spoon until the mixture is completely mixed and smooth again.

Add the sour cream and continue mixing into a stiff paste. If the mixture is too soft, return to the refrigerator for an hour to stiffen.

With a spoon form small balls out of the paste and then roll them in cocoa powder. Shape the truffles according to fancy.

Store in the refrigerator. Allow 15 minutes before serving, once the truffles have been removed from the refrigerator.

Coconut Flan

PREPARATION: 10 MINUTES
COOKING TIME: 50 MINUTES

SERVES: **4**

INGREDIENTS:
5 eggs
3½ oz. grated coconut
3½ oz. fructose
14 fl. oz. whipping
  cream

In a bowl, beat the eggs together with the fructose. Add the whipping cream, and then the coconut.

Pour into a 2 pint cake pan, cover with a cloth and allow to rest for 15 minutes.

Cook for 50 to 60 minutes in a double-boiler in the oven (260°F). Check that the flan is set (insert a skewer into the middle and it should come out clean).

Remove from the oven and allow to cool to room temperature (or until cold) before serving with a raspberry sauce or hot chocolate sauce.

Cream Caramel with Fructose

PREPARATION: 15 MINUTES
COOKING TIME: 55 MINUTES

SERVES: 6

INGREDIENTS:
1¾ pints full cream milk
6 eggs
1 vanilla pod
5 oz. fructose
1 tablespoon cognac

Bring the milk and split vanilla pod slowly to the boil. Allow to cool.

In a mold, heat 2 oz. of fructose with a little water to make a caramel.

In a bowl, beat the eggs with the remaining 3 oz. of fructose. Add the lukewarm milk little by little, beating all the time with the whisk. Add the cognac.

Pour the mixture into the mold and cook for 45 minutes in a fairly hot oven (400°F) in a double-boiler. Allow to cool and then refrigerate for at least 4 hours.

To turn out, place the mold for a few seconds in boiling water. Cover with a plate and turn over quickly. Alternatively, make and serve in individual ramekins.

Cream of Orange

PREPARATION: 20 MINUTES
COOKING TIME: 45 MINUTES

SERVES: 4

INGREDIENTS:
9 egg yolks + 1 whole
    egg
5 oz. fructose
4 or 5 oranges - to give
    about 10 fl. oz. juice
7 fl. oz. whipping cream
zest of 1 orange

Beat together the eggs and the fructose in a large bowl.

Whisk the cream until stiff. Fold into the egg mixture.

Bring the orange juice and zest to the boil and continue boiling for 3 minutes.

Allow to cool for 5 minutes and then pour slowly into the egg mixture, stirring constantly with the whisk.

Pour the mixture into molds and cook in a double-boiler in a pre-heated oven (260°F) for 40 minutes.

Allow to cool and refrigerate for at least 4 to 5 hours before serving.

Fresh Almond Mousse

PREPARATION: 25 MINUTES
COOKING TIME: 15 MINUTES

SERVES: 4-5

INGREDIENTS:
4 eggs
3½ oz. freshly peeled
    almonds
12 fl. oz. very cold
    whipping cream
3½ oz. red currants
3½ oz. fructose powder
juice of ½ lemon
1 teaspoon lemon zest
1 tablespoon liquid
    fructose
mint leaves to decorate

Break the eggs into a bowl and whisk with the fructose in a double-boiler over a low heat. Continue beating till the mixture becomes firm and frothy.

Remove from the double-boiler and continue whisking until the mixture has cooled. Add the lemon juice, the liquid fructose, and the lemon zest. When fully mixed, place on one side and reserve.

Wash the red currants, remove the stalks and dry on kitchen paper.

Chop the almonds. Over a low heat, lightly brown the almonds in a dry non-stick pan.

Whisk the cream until stiff. Fold in the egg mixture and then carefully add the red currants and chopped almonds.

Line the inside of a fluted mold with plastic film. Pour in the mixture and wrap the film over the top.

Refrigerate for 4 hours.

Remove from mold and place onto a plate. Decorate with mint leaves and serve.

Gateau with Fondant Chocolate

PREPARATION: 25 MINUTES
COOKING TIME: 30 MINUTES

SERVES: 4-6

INGREDIENTS:
9 oz. chocolate -
   containing 70%
   cocoa solids
5 eggs
1 teaspoon orange zest
1 pinch salt
2 tablespoons cognac

This dish can be served with whipped cream, vanilla ice cream or with a crème anglaise made with fructose.

Break the eggs and separate the yolks from the whites. Beat the whites with a pinch of salt until stiff.

Melt the chocolate with ½ glass of water in a double-boiler.

Take the pan out of the double-boiler, add the cognac and half of the orange zest. Stir well with a wooden spoon to obtain a very smooth mixture.

Allow to cool for 2 to 3 minutes, then add the egg yolks and mix thoroughly. Fold in the beaten whites until thoroughly mixed. Pour into a greased (8 in.) cake pan which will allow the mixture to settle to a depth of 2 in.

Sprinkle the remaining orange zest over the top.

Cook for 20 minutes in a pre-heated oven (200°F) till the cake is set and a skewer inserted into the center comes out clean.

Grilled Nectarines and Zabaglione

PREPARATION: 15 MINUTES
COOKING TIME: 20 MINUTES

SERVES: 4

INGREDIENTS:
6 good-sized nectarines
5 egg yolks
3½ oz. fructose
7 fl. oz. sparkling white wine

Bring 1½ pints of water to the boil. Add the nectarines and poach for 5 minutes.

Drain and split the nectarines in two, to remove the stones. Then remove the skin and cut each fruit into a total of 8 sections.

Put the egg yolks and the fructose into a large bowl and whisk for 3 or 4 minutes, until they are white and creamy.

To prepare the sabayon, place the bowl with the egg mixture in a double-boiler over a low heat and continue to whisk until the mixture thickens while adding a little wine at regular intervals.

Arrange the nectarines in ovenware dishes. Pour the sabayon over the top and place under the broiler for several minutes before serving.

Grilled Pear Zabaglione

PREPARATION: 20 MINUTES
COOKING TIME: 35 MINUTES

SERVES: 4

INGREDIENTS:
8 large ripe pears
3½ oz. fructose
5 egg yolks
juice of 1 orange
1 teaspoon vanilla
   extract
1 tablespoon rum
mint leaves

This dish can be covered with plastic film and stored in the refrigerator, to be eaten cold or grilled briefly just before serving.

Peel the pears, quarter and remove the cores. Slice each quarter into two.

Arrange the pear slices on the bottom of an ovenware dish lightly brushed with oil. Sprinkle 1 oz. fructose over the top. Place under the broiler for 5 to 10 minutes, to allow the pears to brown lightly without burning. Reserve.

To make the sabayon, whisk the egg yolks and fructose together until they begin to turn slightly white and creamy. Add the orange juice, vanilla, rum and cooking juice from the pears.

Cook gently in a double-boiler, beating constantly, until the cream thickens slightly.

Arrange the pear slices on serving plates. Pour the cream over the top and decorate with a mint leaf.

Lemon Mousse

PREPARATION: 20 MINUTES
COOKING TIME: 20 MINUTES

SERVES: 4

INGREDIENTS:
3 lemons
5 egg yolks + 1 whole egg
7 fl. oz. milk
7 fl. oz. whipping cream
5 oz. fructose
3 leaves gelatin (or equivalent of agar-agar)

Grate the lemon zest.

Beat the eggs with the fructose, juice of 3 lemons, and the lemon zest.

Heat the milk and allow to cool for a few minutes.

Gently pour the milk on the egg and lemon mixture, beating vigorously with a whisk.

Return to a very low heat (preferably in a double-boiler) and allow the mixture to thicken while stirring constantly with the whisk. Allow to cool for 10 minutes.

Soak the leaves of gelatin in cold water for a few minutes. Squeeze dry and add to the mixture, stirring in well with the whisk. Allow to cool for 30 minutes.

Whisk the cream and fold into the mixture. Pour into ramekins brushed with egg white. Cover with plastic film and refrigerate for 5 to 6 hours before serving.

Peaches with Cheese and Raspberries

PREPARATION: 10 MINUTES
COOKING TIME: 10 MINUTES

SERVES: 4

INGREDIENTS:
18 oz. cottage cheese - strained

2 tablespoons sour cream

6 large ripe peaches

3½ oz. sugar-free raspberry jam

mint leaves

Poach the peaches for about 10 minutes. Peel, halve and remove the stones.

Liquefy the cottage cheese, sour cream, and raspberry jam. Pour into the bottom of individual plates. Arrange 3 peach halves on top of each plate. Cover with plastic film and place in the fridge.

Serve chilled and decorate with mint.

Pears in Wine

PREPARATION: 20 MINUTES
COOKING TIME: 20 MINUTES

SERVES: 4

INGREDIENTS:
4 to 6 pears according to size

8 fl. oz. red wine with a high tannin content, like Corbières, Bordeaux, Côtes du Rhône, etc.

3 tablespoons fructose

cinnamon, nutmeg

pepper, pimento (sweet paprika)

Peel the pears and keep the stalk. Place them in a pan, just large enough for them to fit snugly. Add the wine and fructose.

Bring to the boil and cook for 10 minutes with the lid covering about two-thirds of the pan, to ensure the wine does not boil over.

Remove from the heat and turn the pears.

Add 2 or 3 pinches of cinnamon, sweet paprika, grated nutmeg, and freshly ground pepper.

Return to the heat as before and cook for a further 10 minutes.

Check the pears are properly cooked by testing with the sharp point of a knife, and reserve on a separate dish.

Reduce the wine syrup in the casserole to thicken, stirring constantly to avoid it caramelizing on the bottom of the pan.

Arrange the pears in bowls and coat with the syrup.

Raspberry Bavarois with Sauce

PREPARATION: 20 MINUTES
COOKING TIME: 5 MINUTES

SERVES: 4

INGREDIENTS:
1½ lb. raspberries
juice of 1 lemon
3 tablespoons fructose
5 oz. cottage cheese
5 fl. oz. whipping cream
5 leaves gelatin (or the equivalent of agar-agar)

Liquefy the raspberries and put through a conical sieve to remove the pips if necessary.

Drain the cottage cheese.

Add the lemon juice and fructose.

Reserve a third of the mixture in the refrigerator, for making the sauce (coulis) later.

Using a double-boiler, dissolve the gelatin leaves in 2 tablespoons of water and immediately add two-thirds of the raspberry purée. Mix in with the drained cottage cheese and the whipping cream.

Pour into small molds brushed with egg white and refrigerate for 6 hours or until the mixture begins to set.

Remove from molds and serve on individual plates; surround the bavarois with the sauce. Decorate with a mint leaf and serve.

Raspberry Bush

PREPARATION: 20 MINUTES
COOKING TIME: 20 MINUTES

SERVES: 4-5

INGREDIENTS:
8 oz. raspberries
4 egg yolks
18 fl. oz. full cream milk
2 tablespoons fructose
1 vanilla pod
4 leaves gelatin (or equivalent of agar-agar)
7 fl. oz. whipping cream

Split the vanilla pod and add to the milk. Bring the milk slowly to the boil and allow to cool for 10 minutes.

Beat the egg yolks and pour in the milk gradually while continuing to whisk.

Return the mixture to a pan over a very low heat (preferably a double-boiler) and allow to thicken slightly. Stir constantly with a whisk. Add the fructose.

Soak the leaves of gelatin in cold water for a few minutes. Squeeze out and add to the egg mixture, mixing in well with the whisk so that the gelatin dissolves completely. Place on one side and allow to cool for 1 hour.

Whip the cream and fold into the egg mixture before it sets.

Pour the mixture into molds together with the raspberries.

Cover with plastic film and refrigerate for at least 5 or 6 hours.

Serve plain or with whipped cream, sprinkled with cocoa or grated chocolate.

Red Fruit in Red Wine Jelly

PREPARATION: 20 MINUTES
COOKING TIME: 10 MINUTES

SERVES: 6

INGREDIENTS:
7 oz. strawberries

7 oz. raspberries

3½ oz. blueberries

3½ oz. blackberries

14 fl. oz. red wine with a high tannin content, like Corbières, Côtes du Rhône, etc.

3½ fl. oz. liquid fructose (or 4 tablespoons)

½ teaspoon cinnamon

7 leaves gelatin (or the equivalent of agar-agar)

mint leaves

Place a fluted mold in the freezer.

Pour the wine into a pan and add the cinnamon. Bring to the boil and remove immediately from the heat.

Meanwhile, prepare the fruit.

Soften the gelatin for 5 minutes in cold water. Squeeze out and then dissolve in the warm wine. Add the liquid fructose. Stir well and allow to cool.

Take the mold out of the freezer and coat the inside with the wine jelly by tipping the mold from side to side, making sure no part is left uncovered by the jelly.

Return the mold to the freezer for a few minutes and repeat the coating operation until the jelly lining is just under ½ inch in depth all over.

Turn the fruit into the mold. Spread out well using a spoon or spatula and layer of mint leaves.

Pour the rest of the wine jelly carefully over the top and cover with aluminum foil.

Refrigerate overnight or for at least 8 or 10 hours.

Remove from mold just prior to serving.

Rustic Apple Cake

PREPARATION: 25 MINUTES
COOKING TIME: 20 MINUTES

SERVES: 4

INGREDIENTS:
6 or 7 apples
5 oz. fructose
10 eggs + 2 yolks
7 fl. oz. whipping cream
fructose glaze

Quarter, peel, core and slice the apples (about 4 slices per quarter).

Grease a large non-stick pan (8 in. in diameter) with a paper towel soaked in oil.

Arrange the apple slices on the bottom of the pan.

Break the eggs into a bowl. Add the yolks, cream, and half of the fructose. Beat together.

Sprinkle the apples with the rest of the fructose and cook gently until they have lost some of their moisture and are tender.

When the apples are soft and slightly transparent, add the egg mixture and continue to cook.

When two-thirds of the omelette has cooked, put the pan under the broiler to complete the cooking and make the top golden-brown.

Sprinkle the top with the fructose glaze and serve.

Strawberries with Mint and Yogurt

PREPARATION: 15 MINUTES
NO COOKING

SERVES: 4

INGREDIENTS:
1½ lb. strawberries
3 containers (4 oz. each), plain yogurt
1 large bunch of mint
2 tablespoons of sugar-free strawberry jam

Rinse, drain on kitchen paper and remove the stalks from the strawberries. Arrange in small bowls.

Remove the mint leaves from their stems and chop finely.

In a bowl, mix the yogurt, chopped mint and strawberry jam. Chill in the refrigerator.

Pour the yogurt sauce over the strawberries and serve.

Strawberries with Orange and Mint

PREPARATION: 10 MINUTES
COOKING TIME: 15 MINUTES

SERVES: 4

INGREDIENTS:
1 lb. strawberries

3 oranges

½ glass Cointreau

1½ oz. fructose

12 leaves mint

Squeeze the juice out of the oranges.

Put the orange juice, Cointreau, fructose, and 5 of the chopped mint leaves into a small pan. Bring to the boil and reduce by half. Allow to cool.

Rinse the strawberries under the faucet and drain on kitchen paper.

Remove the stalks from the berries and cut into halves.

Arrange on individual plates.

Coat with the minted orange syrup.

Decorate with the remaining mint leaves and serve.

USEFUL ADDRESSES

Erica House Publishing
P.O.Box 1109
Frederick, MD 21702

Websites:

www.EatYourselfSlim.com

www.MontignacUSA.com

www.EricaHouse.com

e-mail:editor@montignacusa.com

Montignac Nutrition & Vitality Centers
1116 S.Fort Harrison Avenue
Clearwater, FL 33756

e-mail:Montignac@usa.com